"For those individuals early in sobriety, still struggling with their recovery, this book provides a gentle introduction to spirituality and the Twelve Steps. It touches on the heart of each Step and lights the path to a more loving, peaceful way of life."

Susan Schavi, Rehabilitation Therapist, Addictions Services Division of Connecticut Valley Hospital, Middletown, CT

"At last, a book on how to identify and practice one of the most elusive states of being. Spirituality is demystified in this practical guide for the Twelve Step beginner and therapist alike."

Sherry Baxter, Therapist, formerly Rehabilitation Counselor for Connecticut Department of Corrections, and Assistant Directors for both Daniel Casriel Institute and Samaritan HalfWay Society in New York City

About the Author

Gregg D., a recovering alcoholic, is a writer, poet, and university instructor, as well as a gifted speaker on the spiritual nature of recovery from alcoholism and addictions. Gregg has been an active part of the recovering communities in Florida, Virginia, and Connecticut, and currently resides in a Sufi community in upstate New York. His professional career has taken him from a Washington law practice to international law and investment banking. Today, in addition to Twelfth Step service work, Gregg remains in service to his community assisting with abused and neglected children through court appointments and foster care.

Gregg D. is available to lead workshops and week-end retreats to introduce or enhance the spiritual aspects of the Twelve Step recovery program, creating the opportunity for an experiential practice of the principles leading to a spiritual awakening.

To contact Gregg or receive further information on workshops and retreats, please write to:

Awakened Recoveries
P. O. Box 48
Richmond, MA 01254
www.awakened-recoveries.net

D0916425

The Spirituality of Sobriety

Finding the Spiritual Awakening in Recovery from Alcoholism

Gregg D.

Cover design and art by Sherry Baxter, Torrington, CT.

Published by Awakened Recoveries, P. O. Box 48, Richmond, MA 01254
www.awakened-recoveries.net

ISBN: 0-9754106-0-1

Printed by Edwards Brothers, Inc.
http://www.edwardsbrothers.com

Contents

Introduction

This book is not intended to be a companion workbook to the Twelve Steps of Alcoholics Anonymous. Its purpose is not to assist the newcomer to A.A. in working his way through the Steps in the early period of his recovery. There are plenty of great books already on the shelves that cover that ground. I used them myself.

Rather, this book is simply the overflowing of my own recovery. I have received so much from attending A.A. meetings and studying the A.A. literature that the stuff just bubbles up inside me now. I hear one particular thing shared at a meeting, find it connecting with something I read in the literature that week, then remember something else about it from elsewhere in the literature or from something somebody told me, and then I find myself continuing to chew the thing for the rest of the week. By the time it's finished feeding me my dose of personal recovery, I find I have way too much left over to share at a meeting. So I share bits of it, and talk in more depth with my friends in recovery. People often thanked me for sharing, and asked questions. Hearing other approaches from friends brought my own thinking into more clarity. And then, one day, I started gathering the pieces together in the recovery themes that had come to me. I sat with that material for over a year. And then, one day, I started writing chapters.

You will find much of the A.A. literature of recovery in this book. Our two basic texts are *Alcoholics Anonymous: The Story of How Many Thousands of Men and Women Have Recovered from Alcoholism*,[1] and *Twelve Steps and Twelve Traditions*.[2] A.A. members refer to the first text as the *Big Book,* and the second as the *Twelve and Twelve.* The *Big Book* has been recently published in a fourth edition. The basic text has remained the same, but new stories have been added. The *Big Book* was

---

[1]Third Edition (New York: Alcoholics Anonymous World Services, 1976).
[2](New York: Alcoholics Anonymous World Services, 1953).

The Spirituality of Sobriety

written and edited by Bill Wilson and the early members of A.A. and initially published in 1939, only four years after the beginning of A.A. "To show other alcoholics *precisely how we have recovered* is the main purpose of this book."[3] It is the original documentation of the development and success of the Twelve Steps used as a program of recovery for alcoholism. The Twelve Steps are reprinted in the Appendix. The *Twelve and Twelve*, initially published 14 years later, is based on the early experience of individual A.A. members and groups confronting issues that arose in working their way through the recovery program laid out in the *Big Book*. "This present volume proposes to broaden and deepen the understanding of the Twelve Steps as first written in the earlier work."[4] As such, the *Twelve and Twelve* is more directly focused on the Steps in the recovery program initially presented in the *Big Book* and provides specific guidance for each of them.

When we start into recovery, it is strongly recommended that we ask someone of our choosing to "sponsor" us. The purpose of sponsoring is to provide the newcomer with someone who can introduce him to the meetings and the people, and get him started on the early issues of recovery. He is a person with whom the newcomer can share his problems in more detail than may be appropriate at an A.A. meeting. As we say, "Our stories disclose in a *general way* ...."[5] Often, the sponsor provides more specific guidance that helps the newcomer grow in his sobriety. Later, the newcomer may find himself sharing with others the bits of wisdom and practical advise his sponsor shared with him at times of crisis in his life. The circumstances during my early recovery made sponsorship difficult for me. While I had several people that sponsored me, our contact was too erratic to form the firm basis of my recovery. I was traveling overseas for my job too much to get the consistent contact. In addition, I had four geographical job relocations in my first few years of recovery. And three times I have had sponsors move across country from me.

---

[3] *Big Book*, at p. xiii.
[4] *Twelve and Twelve*, at p. 17.
[5] *Big Book*, at p. 58 (emphasis added).

So, the A.A. literature itself became the firm basis for my recovery. Where many recovering alcoholics are likely to quote their sponsor, I am more likely to quote a passage from the literature. While I carry some precious truths given to me by my sponsors in the past, the wealth of recovery wisdom that kept me going on a day-by-day basis came from A.A. literature. While I was flying in airplanes, I was reading the *Big Book*. When I was overnight in a hotel, after checking in with the local A.A. answering service, and maybe being lucky enough to find my way to an A.A. meeting in a strange town, I would study the *Twelve and Twelve*. It was this reading and studying that kept me away from a drink on the road. The words in the texts came alive for me – it was as if they had been written just for me. When I was able to attend an A.A. meeting, I would then hear the sharing in this context of my own reading, and the sharing took on much depth for me. I would begin to see the principles in the texts inside the stories shared at the meeting. The stories would then open facets of the principle to me, and I would see in new light something I had previously read in the texts.

I do not know if the A.A. literature is a scripture. Perhaps it is for the alcoholic seeking recovery from his drinking! But the literature has certainly worked like scripture for me in the way it comes alive for me. Some do believe the texts are inspired by God. Whether or not the A.A. literature was inspired, the texts certainly are the written record of desperate and dying men and women who found the God of their understanding in a way perhaps only an alcoholic can. The literature may become scripture for the alcoholic in this sense: that it is the written record of a group of men and women who found their way out of a fatal disease, to healing, life and a spiritual awakening, and they wrote down the specific directions so we coming later can follow the way they had traveled. That sounds like scripture to me. But then, I am one of those desperate alcoholics.

Finally, please keep in mind that this book is merely a reflection of the things I have gleaned over the years from the A.A. literature and the sharing in meetings that have become the recovery wisdom that kept me away from a drink while growing in sobriety. You may well have read the same passages in the course of your recovery and gleaned a different understanding which has kept you sober today. And when you share that bit of recovery wisdom in a meeting and I hear it, it may become just the thing that keeps me sober for the next day. That was the understanding of the authors of the *Big Book*: "Our book is meant to be suggestive only. We realize we know only a little. God will constantly disclose more to you and to us."[6] That is the way it works, and keeps working, in recovery. The whole program began with one alcoholic talking to another, and it continues today in the same way. We have found that what we cannot do alone, we can do together. God Bless.

---

[6] *Big Book*, at p. 164.

Chapter 1
Recovery as a Spiritual Experience

*"Came to believe that a Power greater than
ourselves could restore us to sanity."*

Step Two

My name is Gregg. I'm alcoholic. That's how I introduce myself at the
A.A. meetings I still attend regularly. Alcoholics Anonymous. That's where I
found sobriety, stopped drinking, got into recovery and found my life again.
Got my health back. My thinking cleared up. And, I found a deep spirituality
that has taken hold of me by the roots of my soul. It is the story of this
spirituality in sobriety that I would like to tell now. What it is for me and
how it has come about.

We are often asked to share our "story" in A.A. The story is usually
about too much drinking over some period of years, with the inevitable
problems with spouses, family, work and the law; followed by some crisis
or intervention; then a period of drying out; and, finally, a second chance at
life through attendance at A.A. meetings. But it seems to me there could be
much more about this story. While I always identify with the drinking
stories ("what we used to be like"), and I enjoy hearing about what
happened to start the sobriety process ("what happened"), I also long to
hear more about what a recovering alcoholic's life is like now ("what we
are like now").[1] I want to hear about the *good* stuff. I want to know there is
good stuff there waiting for me, and I want to know how to get it.

---

[1] *Big Book*, at p. 58.

The Spirituality of Sobriety

Because our stories so often focused on the drinking and the cessation of drinking, I thought this was what A.A. was all about. My first clue that it might be about something more came to me while sitting in an early meeting where the Twelve Steps hung as a banner from the wall. I noticed the word "alcohol" only appeared in the First Step and then was never mentioned again. The Steps did not seem to talk about, or address alcohol or drinking. Rather, they talked a lot about admissions, inventories, power and powerlessness, character defects, amends, prayer and spiritual awakenings.

What about our literature? Certainly the *Big Book* and the *Twelve and Twelve* would be focused on telling me about alcohol and how to stop drinking. Yet the books seemed to be full of other stuff, including God and spirituality. "Well, that's exactly what this book is about," says the *Big Book*. "Its main object is to enable you to find a Power greater than yourself which will solve your problem. That means we have written a book which we believe to be spiritual as well as moral."[2] I thought the *Big Book's* "main object" would be to enable me to find a way to stop drinking, yet by the author's own admission, the book's intent and purpose is to guide me to a higher power along some spiritual path. The *Twelve and Twelve* was no better. Its Introduction boldly states that "A.A.'s Twelve Steps are a group of principles, spiritual in nature...."[3] These are not simple steps for drying out enforced by the professional staff at a detox/rehabilitation center. The very principles of A.A., we are told, "were borrowed mainly from the fields of religion and medicine,"[4] not just medicine and psychiatry. No wonder there is so much more than just references to alcohol and drinking in the A.A. literature.

What about the meetings? Certainly this would be about alcohol and how to stop drinking. However, as recounted in the *Big Book*, the first meetings were "to be attended by anyone or everyone interested in a

---

[2] *Big Book*, at p. 45.
[3] *Twelve and Twelve*, at p. 15.
[4] *Big Book*, at p. 16.

spiritual way of life."[5] The "prime object" of the meeting "was to provide a time and place where new people might bring their problems."[6] Again, I would have thought the "prime object" of the meeting would be to talk about alcohol and how to stop drinking, and that people attending would be alcoholics, not some form of spiritual seekers.

So, why all this insistence on God and spiritual stuff? Why not just talk about alcohol and tell me how to stop drinking? Well, it seems that approach might work for me if I just had a problem of drinking too much alcohol sometimes. The literature is not insistent upon a spiritual experience in order for a problem drinker to stop drinking. "Whether such a person can quit upon a nonspiritual basis depends upon the extent to which he has already lost the power to choose whether he will drink or not."[7] But, if I am an alcoholic, a "real" alcoholic as the *Big Book* describes him, then I have lost the power within myself to quit, or even control, my drinking.[8] So, knowledge about alcohol and methods to stop drinking are not enough for me. I had already tried plenty of "self-help" methods for abstinence, and failed. If A.A. is simply one more method for "me" to stop drinking, then it, too, will fail.

Since the real alcoholic has lost the ability on his own power to stop drinking, he must find a power greater than himself to help him stop. And this search is likely to be the beginning of a spiritual journey for him. As a real alcoholic, I "may be suffering from an illness which only a spiritual experience will conquer."[9] Even more decisively, for the real alcoholic, the *Big Book* says "we must find a spiritual basis of life – or else."[10] His recovery "is dependent upon his relationship with God," and the only condition to his recovery "is that he trust God and clean house."[11]

Well, if my recovery is going to be about God and spirituality, then how come the A.A. meeting is not a prayer meeting or a Bible study, and how come the literature is not some form of sacred text about God and angels and miracles? These sorts of activities may become part of my life and

[5] *Big Book*, at p. 159-60.
[6] *Big Book*, at p. 160.
[7] *Big Book*, at p. 34.
[8] *Big Book*, at p. 44.
[9] *Big Book*, at p. 44.
[10] *Big Book*, at p. 44
[11] *Big Book*, at p. 98

The Spirituality of Sobriety

recovery, but they will occur outside of A.A. In the course of the Eleventh
Step, we are invited, even encouraged, to seek out places of worship and to
return to former religious connections and practices.[12] But the spirituality
of sobriety is much simpler and much more focused than the concepts and
practices of the various religious traditions. First of all, there is very little
about belief or doctrines of faith in this spirituality. Rather, we find it is
about knowledge and action. Second, there is little about heaven and
eternity, but much about this world and the present. Third, there is little
about the nature of God and the unchangeable absolute, but much about
the nature of the alcoholic and the absolute necessity for change.

So, should I join a religious order and pray and meditate every day
until I have visions of angels and become one with all in the universe?
These may be good things to be doing. But, I may have visions of angels and
still drink myself silly every night.

The spiritual experience that my recovery from alcoholism depends
upon is a bit different. It tends to be more about me, my problems, and the
solution. The *Big Book* describes the spiritual experience required for
recovery as "huge emotional displacements and rearrangements. Ideas,
emotions, and attitudes which were once the guiding forces of the lives of
these men are suddenly cast to one side, and a completely new set of
conceptions and motives begin to dominate them."[13] This spirituality is
experiential resulting in significant changes in my emotions and attitudes.
My very responses to life situations change. I feel differently about things,
and I react differently. I connect with people around me in new ways. The
Twelve and Twelve confirms that this spiritual awakening is about the
alcoholic becoming "able to do, feel, and believe that which he could not
do before on his unaided strength and resources alone."[14] I found I was at
last able to act like an adult and fully feel the emotions of a normal human
being without overreacting to everything. This practical type of spiritual
experience leaves the recovering alcoholic "in possession of a degree of

---

[12] *Twelve and Twelve*, at p. 98.
[13] *Big Book*, at p. 27.
[14] *Twelve and Twelve*, at p. 107.

honesty, tolerance, unselfishness, peace of mind, and love of which he had thought himself quite incapable."[15]

A lot of the good qualities I now find in my life first appeared as a result of the spiritual awakening, but these changes may show up in my life in a more gradual way. Although sometimes the alcoholic may feel "rocketed into a fourth dimension of existence,"[16] my own experience was a more gradual spiritual awakening. I was at first not even aware of it. My friends first saw the change, and only later did I become aware of "a profound alteration in [my] reaction to life."[17] While not as dramatic as some spiritual experiences may be, this type of spiritual awakening will form the basis of a solid recovery for the alcoholic.

This spirituality of sobriety is not based on doctrines of faith. But doesn't the Second Step, "Came to believe that a Power greater than ourselves could restore us to sanity," require some admission of faith? The only admissions required of the Steps are the admission of powerlessness in Step One and the admission of our wrongs in Step Five. No admission of faith is required in Step Two. "Alcoholics Anonymous does not demand that you believe anything. All of its Twelve Steps are but suggestions."[18] The Second Step is stated in a passive tense. We are not actively asserting some belief or profession of faith. There are no catechisms here. In response to concerns of some that A.A. may require conformity to some form of faith, Bill Wilson wrote: "They just don't realize that faith is never a necessity for A.A. membership; that sobriety can be achieved with an easily acceptable minimum of it; and that our concepts of a higher power and God as we understand him afford everyone a nearly unlimited choice of spiritual belief and action."[19] I have always enjoyed the advice frequently heard in A.A. meetings on the Second Step that there are only two things I need to believe about God – first, that there is one, and second, that I'm not it!

Our Western religious traditions tend to emphasize the object of our faith over the practice of that faith. The early origins of Christianity's

---

[15] *Twelve and Twelve*, at p. 107.
[16] *Big Book*, at p. 25.
[17]*Big Book*, at p. 569 (Appendix II).

[18] *Twelve and Twelve*, at p. 26 (Step Two).
[19] *The Language of the Heart* (New York: The AA Grapevine, 1988), at p. 251.

diversity of theology on the nature of God and Jesus culminated in the Nicene Creed in 324 A.D. The Council of Nicea was called by the first converted Roman emperor to resolve disputes and schisms within the early Church over doctrines of faith. The Creed itself is stated in repeated terms of "we believe *in*...." We believe *in* one God..., we believe *in* one Lord, Jesus Christ..., we believe *in* the Holy Spirit..., etc. Church history is replete with continuing enforcement efforts over these doctrines of faith, including the Inquisition, wars, and crusades against "heretics." I find it of great significance that our Second Step is not stated in terms of a belief *in* anything. Rather, the Second Step speaks of a belief *that*.... The Second Step simply makes an affirmative statement of faith about a capability held by the Higher Power, *i.e.*, that He is capable of restoring us to sanity. The faith found in the Second Step does not address the nature of the Higher Power we find. This understanding is left to the consciousness of the individual recovering alcoholic.

It is through the admission of powerlessness in the First Step that we find faith in a Higher Power. In other words, we do not come to belief by a profession of blind faith in God, but rather by an admission of powerlessness in ourselves. Because I am convinced at Step One that I no longer have the power on my own to beat the obsession to drink, and because the need to be free of the obsession has become so urgent, I am forced to seek elsewhere for a power greater than my obsession, and in seeking I find. "Step Two is the rallying point for all of us."[20] In total retreat from my alcoholism in Step One, I find the rallying point to stop the retreat at Step Two.

In my desperation, I am not concerned so much about my conception of the nature of the Higher Power – I just need enough of something to get started. The point of the Second Step is not to achieve the correct, orthodox view of God, but rather to make a meaningfully real contact with Him. "Our own conception, however inadequate, was sufficient to make the approach

---

[20] *Twelve and Twelve*, at p. 33.

and to effect a contact with Him."[21] It is this real contact that will start the process of relieving my obsession to drink, not some catechism of correct doctrines of faith. And then the faith develops more. "Relieved of the alcohol obsession, their lives unaccountably transformed, they came to believe in a Higher Power."[22] My faith is based on facts – my own experience of power and life changes. Our belief itself is the result, not the cause, of change we begin to see happening to us.

The unique approach to faith in the Second Step is the reason why a philosophical atheist or agnostic can quite easily find himself moving into the spirituality of sobriety. "Surprisingly enough, we find such [agnostic] convictions no great obstacle to a spiritual experience."[23] On the other hand, and perhaps even more surprising, "religious convictions" may not always constitute "the necessary vital spiritual experience," that will relieve our alcoholism.[24] Rumi, a Thirteenth-Century Sufi mystic poet, wrote of this distinction between doctrines of faith and the spiritual experience:

I have given each being a separate and unique way
of seeing and knowing and saying that knowledge.

What seems wrong to you is right for him.
What is poison to one is honey to someone else.
Purity and impurity, sloth and diligence in worship,
these mean nothing to me. I am apart from all that.

Ways of worshiping are not to be ranked as better
or worse. Hindus do Hindu things. The Dravidian
Muslims in India do what they do. It's all praise,
and it's all right. I am not glorified in acts

of worship. It's the worshipers! I don't hear
the words they say. I look inside at the humility.

[21] *Big Book*, at p. 46.
[22] *Twelve and Twelve*, at p. 28.
[23] *Big Book*, at p. 28-29.
[24] *Big Book*, at p. 27.

That broken-open lowliness is the reality. Forget
phraseology! I want burning, burning.[25]

It is not about a certain belief or faith in a concept, but rather about my
own individual experience facing my own powerlessness and finding a new
power greater than myself. "We begin to feel the nearness of our Creator.
We may have had certain spiritual beliefs, but now we begin to have a
spiritual experience."[26] We find we are able to make use of the spiritual
principles of the recovery program without concern or regard for articles
of faith, and that the principles nonetheless work.[27]

This is the part of the recovering alcoholic's story that I long to hear –
the good stuff, the really good stuff. It is from this kind of a spiritual
experience in other alcoholics that I can come to believe that the same
thing can happen to me. At anniversary meetings, the celebrants are often
asked how they stayed sober for another year. The typical answer is: "We
keep it real simple. We just don't drink and we go to meetings." Imagine
the spiritual awakening across the entire room if the celebrants' answer
instead was:

> The great fact is just this, and nothing less: That we have had deep
> and effective spiritual experiences which have revolutionized our
> whole attitude toward life, toward our fellows and toward God's
> universe. The central fact of our lives today is the absolute
> certainty that our Creator has entered into our hearts and lives in
> a way which is indeed miraculous. He has commenced to
> accomplish those things for us which we could never do by
> ourselves.[28]

If I have not personally had this kind of spiritual experience, then there is
much more in the recovery program for me to receive. If I have had this
kind of spiritual experience, then it simply has to be a major part of my
story. And so, now, I would like to tell the story of this spirituality in
sobriety – what it is for me, and how it has come about.

---

[25] Coleman Barks, tr., *The Book of Love*
(New York: HarperCollins Publishers,
2003), at pp. 166-67.

[26] *Big Book*, at p. 75.
[27] *Big Book*, at p. 47.
[28] *Big Book*, at p. 25.

Chapter 2
The Spiritual Awakening

"Having had a spiritual awakening
as the result of these steps. ..."

Step Twelve

I come into recovery beaten by alcohol and desperately seeking a solution to the obsession to drink that has destroyed me physically, mentally, emotionally, financially, and spiritually. I am instructed in the Twelve Steps, and begin to actually do the work suggested by this program. Time goes by and one day I find that I have had "a spiritual awakening as the result of these steps." I did not come into recovery seeking a spiritual awakening, and I did not think I was taking on a religious practice to bring about a spiritual awakening. I did not attend to the teachings or discipline of a spiritual master, or become inducted or initiated into any religious group or tradition. I simply attended A.A. meetings, listened to a lot of other alcoholics, took guidance in working the Steps from others in the program, did the work, and managed to stay sober long enough for the compulsion to drink to lift. And then I had a spiritual awakening.

There is great irony in this. Recovering alcoholics are not the only ones having spiritual awakenings in the world today. Many undergo a conversion experience at the hand of an evangelist, or receive direct transmission from a Hindu master. Westerners have taken to yoga and forms of Buddhist meditation in great numbers seeking to achieve spiritual awakenings. People are studying chakras, Buddhist theology, and New Age

The Spirituality of Sobriety

esoteric metaphysics. The mystical aspects of Christianity, Judaism and Islam all draw people hungering today for spiritual awakening. Rumi, the Sufi mystic poet, is one of the best selling poets in America today.

While everyone was busy about all this study and discipline seeking a spiritual awakening, what was I doing? Drinking myself silly every night for 20 years, wrecking a perfectly fine marriage and family, and thoroughly numbing out to all life – here or hereafter. Whipped by alcoholism, I am introduced to recovery by a therapist and begin to follow the suggestions for how to get through a day without finding it necessary to drink. And the result? A spiritual awakening. I will say it again: There is great irony in this.

"Our Twelfth Step… says that as a result of practicing all the Steps, we have each found something called a spiritual awakening. To new A.A.'s, this often seems like a very dubious and improbable state of affairs."[1] It certainly seemed that way to me. I would have thought the Twelfth Step would have said that as the result of practicing all the steps, we have found *sobriety*. When I started into recovery, I thought sobriety was my goal. It still seems to me that should have been the goal. Yet the literature says the result of the alcoholic's practice of the Steps is a definite, conclusive spiritual awakening "about which finally there [is] no question."[2] My own experience confirms this. At the same time, I have also remained sober and continue to do so. I now realize the spiritual awakening and on-going sobriety have become powerfully and wonderfully linked together. I have found that as I work toward either one, the other also occurs for me, with profound synergy between the awakening and the sobriety.

For me, this spiritual awakening has opened me in a number of ways. My point of view has changed significantly. Before, I always seemed to be in the center of the circle, with all points on the circumference relating directly to me like spokes on a wheel connecting to the hub. Now, I see myself as just one more point on the circumference. I can now see people, things and events in relationship to other things, not necessarily in

---

[1] *Twelve and Twelve*, at p. 106.
[2] *Twelve and Twelve*, at p. 109.

relationship to me. I can hear someone else share something without assuming it is about me, in response to me, or a criticism of me. Where I used to repel people away from me, or wish they would go away, I now find I am often drawn toward people and may be drawing them towards me. I am not so insistent upon my way, and I seem to have more tolerance and patience with people around me since I find them all so incredibly interesting. My first awakening to this heightened attraction to people occurred in an airport early in recovery. I was walking alone down a wide corridor toward a section of gates when a few planes began deboarding at the same time. Hundreds of people filled the corridor and came streaming towards me. In the past this would have upset me because I never enjoyed crowds. This time, as I stood watching them come, I was flooded with a sense of awe and wonder and love toward all the people I saw – individually and collectively. My reaction had completely changed.

An aspect of this feeling is simply the acceptance that often forms the topic of an A.A. meeting.

Acceptance is the answer to *all* my problems today. When I am disturbed, it is because I find some person, place, thing, or situation – some fact of my life – unacceptable to me, and I can find no serenity until I accept that person, place, thing, or situation as being exactly the way it is supposed to be at this moment. Nothing, absolutely nothing happens in God's world by mistake. Until I could accept my alcoholism, I could not stay sober; unless I accept life completely on life's terms, I cannot be happy.[3]

Often this acceptance is sought as a means of relieving an emotional disturbance arising over my insistence that people, places and things conform to my expectations. I discover that many of my problems in life are simply the result of my unreasonable expectations of others. I find the

---

[3] *Big Book*, at p. 449.

solution to these problems by releasing my expectations of others and accepting people, places and things exactly the way they are at the moment. My first year of recovery was an almost constant exercise in learning to "accept the things I cannot change," as our Serenity Prayer[4] says.

However, the acceptance that I find in the spiritual awakening is not about solving my own emotional disturbance. Rather, this acceptance seems to arise from a deep sense of wonder and awe and love for people simply as people. This deeper, "awakened" acceptance of a particular person has been wonderfully described by the psychologist Carl Rogers as "a warm regard for him as a person of unconditional self-worth – of value no matter what his condition, his behavior, or his feelings. It means a respect and liking for him as a separate person, a willingness for him to possess his own feelings in his own way."[5] I have come to refer to this as "radical acceptance." It goes way beyond simply releasing my expectations of others. I now attempt the next step of affirmatively accepting each person for no reason other than his mere existence. I try to look past the particular condition, behavior or feelings to the deeper awareness of the person and extend to him this warm regard. I try to interact with the person based on a belief in his unconditional self-worth unrelated to anything he does, says or believes himself.

From here, this radical acceptance of people, places and things can blossom into a spiritual experience. A young poet killed in World War I captured this more mystical aspect of acceptance in wonderful words:

> Do not leap or turn pale at the word Mysticism, I do not mean any religious thing or any form of belief.
>
> It consists just in looking at people and things as themselves – neither as useful nor moral nor ugly nor anything else; but just as being. At least, that is a philosophical description of it. What happens is that I suddenly feel the extraordinary value and importance of everybody I meet, and almost everything I see. In

---

[4] See Appendix, Prayers in Recovery
[5] Carl Rogers, *On Becoming A Person* (Boston: Houghton Mifflin Company, 1961), at p. 34.

22

things I am moved in this way, especially by some things; but in people by almost all people. That is, when the mood is on me. I roam about places – yesterday I did it even in Birmingham! – and I sit in trains and see the essential glory and beauty of all the people I meet. I can watch a dirty middle-aged tradesman in a railway-carriage for hours, and love every dirty greasy sulky wrinkle in his weak chin and every button on his spotted unclean waistcoat. I know their states of mind are bad. But I'm so much occupied with their being there at all, that I don't have time to think of it. I tell you that a Birmingham gouty Tariff Reform fifth rate business-man is splendid and immortal and desirable.

It's the same about the things of ordinary life. Half an hour's roaming about a street or village or railway-station shows so much beauty that it's impossible to be anything but wild with suppressed exhilaration. And it's not only beauty and beautiful things. In a flicker of sunlight on a blank wall, or a reach of muddy pavement, or smoke from an engine at night, there's a sudden significance and importance and inspiration that makes the breath stop with a gulp of certainty and happiness. It's not that the wall or the smoke seem important for anything or suddenly reveal any general statement, or are suddenly seen to be good or beautiful in themselves – only that *for you* they're perfect and unique. It's like being in love with a person. . . . I suppose my occupation is being in love with the universe.[6]

In this way, any place can become holy in itself, and any event can easily become a spiritual experience. It is not that other people change for the better. I simply awake to their presence at a deeper level and begin to engage with them from that perspective.

---

[6] Personal Letter of Rupert Brooke, quoted in Colin Wilson, *Poetry & Mysticism* (San Francisco: City Lights Books, 1969), at pp. 120-21.

The Spirituality of Sobriety

A similar experience sometimes occurs when I do see a greater significance seeming to lie behind people and things. Rather than the radical acceptance of people, places and things just as they are at the moment, I sometimes feel as if God is standing just behind the person, place or thing and I catch Him peeking out from behind His creation. A Jesuit poet/priest of the late nineteenth century saw the grandeur of God behind created things, and spoke of it this way:

> The world is charged with the grandeur of God,
> It will flame out, like shining from shook foil;
> It gathers to a greatness, like the ooze of oil....[7]

While I was visiting family in Switzerland, I was awestruck by the immediacy and towering presence of the Alps coming into view as a heavy fog lifted in the morning sun. The Alps had been there all the time, I just was unable to see them through the fog that covered my eyes of perception. It is like that, the sudden awareness of a presence that had been there all the time, but only now, with some immediacy, coming into my awareness. Playing off Moses' experience with the burning bush in the Bible, Elizabeth Barrett Browning almost shouts her revelation of this experience:

> Earth's crammed with heaven,
> And every common bush afire with God;
> But only he who sees, takes off his shoes –
> The rest sit round it and pluck blackberries,
> And daub their natural faces unaware....[8]

Most days I join the crowd eating blackberries. But on a particular day, with a mood I cannot describe in words, I sometimes see the bush afire,

---

[7] Gerard Manley Hopkins, *God's Grandeur.*
[8] Elizabeth Barrett Browning, *Aurora Leigh, Seventh Book.*

and I have the spiritual experience of "taking off my shoes" in awe of the sense of eternity embedded in all of creation.

William Wordsworth captured this same mood in his *Lines Composed A Few Miles Above Tintern Abbey*:

> And I have felt
> A presence that disturbs me with the joy
> Of elevated thoughts; a sense sublime
> Of something far more deeply interfused,
> Whose dwelling is the light of setting suns,
> And the round ocean and the living air,
> And the blue sky, and in the mind of man;
> A motion and a spirit, that impels
> All thinking things, all objects of all thought,
> And rolls through all things.[9]

This is the majestic sense of greatness behind the veil of something I see. Another well-known Romantic poet, William Blake, believed man had restricted himself to what he called single vision, and so had lost the ability to truly perceive the spiritual presence behind the things of this world:

> To see a World in a Grain of Sand
> And a Heaven in a Wild Flower
> Hold Infinity in the palm of your hand
> And Eternity in an hour[10]

Blake felt the problem was with our distorted sense of perception:

> If the doors of perception were cleansed every thing would appear to man as it is: infinite.

---

[9] William Wordsworth, *Lines Composed A Few Miles Above Tintern Abbey*.
[10] William Blake, *Auguries of Innocence*.

The Spirituality of Sobriety

> For man has closed himself up, till he sees all things thro'
> narrow chinks of his cavern.[11]

Part of the spiritual awakening for me seems to be a change in my perception so that I see more than the mere physical image conveyed to my eye. The deeper, broader meaning of the image becomes clear to me, carrying hints of heaven and the infinite.

A wonderful aspect of this awakening occurs when I experience the sense of union with this ultimate significance behind the everyday events. It is an interrupting of my own life in honor of something greater arriving. Of course my plans change when this greater presence is announced! I first saw this in a practical way on I-95. A violent accident involving two cars happened in morning rush hour less than a mile ahead of me in my plain view. Both cars had rolled off the highway into the median. By the time I came up to them, many people had already pulled over and were helping people out of the vehicles and caring for them. I had the sudden realization that all the people who stopped had had something important to do and were moving with purpose in a particular direction just seconds before the crash. After the crash, their own plans paled in significance to the tragedy that called for their help. I thought of the morning business appointments missed, the important presentation that would not be made that morning, people elsewhere waiting for the late arrival of these Good Samaritans. Those who stopped to help became joined together in a union with an event (albeit a tragic one) that had more significance than any of their own individual plans for the day. It is this union of which I speak, the sense of recognizing the greater importance of an incident and taking on the activities required of it in place of my own individual plans. This same sense of union occurs some days for me with the simple awareness of the sunrise and that God has work in the universe that is greater than my little plans for the day. It is the union of my taking on the work associated with

---

[11] William Blake, *The Marriage of Heaven and Hell.*

something greater than me as if it were my own work. Large events replace my small activities and I move into union with something greater than myself. "Established on such a footing we became less and less interested in ourselves, our little plans and designs. More and more we became interested in seeing what we could contribute to life."[12]

There is also a paradox that arises for me in the spiritual awakening. As I come into the awakening, I have a strong realization that "none of this is about me." I see my own insignificance in light of the larger vision of a universe beyond my capacity to understand. The things that are going on in this universe are much bigger than I am. And these large events will continue whether I am around or not. And then the paradox: Part of the spiritual awakening for me becomes a strong sense that "it *is* all about me." The purpose and intent of the entire universe seems to come home to me. It is the overwhelming sense of a great loving presence directing attention toward *me*. I feel myself the object of an affection that overwhelms my personality and catches hold of me at the deepest core of my heart. And in the presence of this love, there is a deep realization of the importance of a human being and of my own importance as one in whom life flows.

> O I could sing such grandeurs and glories about you!
> You have not known what you are, you have slumber'd upon
>   yourself all your life,
> Your eyelids have been the same as closed most of the time,
> What you have done returns already in mockeries....
>
> The mockeries are not you.
> Underneath them and within them I see you lurk,
> I pursue you where none else has pursued you....
> As for me, I give nothing to any one except I give the like
>   carefully to you,

---

[12] *Big Book*, at p. 63.

The Spirituality of Sobriety

> I sing the songs of the glory of none, not God, sooner than I
> sing the songs of the glory of you.[13]

It is this ultimate sense of belonging that the *Twelve and Twelve* finds to be the greatest reward of meditation and prayer in the Eleventh Step: "We know that God lovingly watches over us. We know that when we turn to Him, all will be well with us, here and hereafter."[14]

When I was still drinking, I can remember wanting to be able to walk into a room and make no impact at all, because I was having such a negative impact on everything around me at that time. I was like the man in the Third Step discussion in the *Big Book*: "Is he not, even in his best moments, a producer of confusion rather than harmony?"[15] Part of my spiritual awakening was the taking of responsibility for the energy I was putting out to those around me. I realized energy did flow from me, as a human being, and I was certainly contributing to the atmosphere around me. My drunken wish of having no impact was not possible. As a human being, I had impact, I was bringing something to the party. The only question is, "What was I bringing?" And the awakening revealed to me the great responsibility I had to assure that the energy I put out was good and beneficial. Now I walk into a room, and I pray I do have an impact. I sincerely hope that things are different in the room because I walked into it. I hope the energy flowing from me has contributed to an atmosphere of peace and contentment and lovingkindness to those in the room.

A Buddhist master defined spiritual awakening as seeing the goodness in yourself. In working the Steps, I find powerlessness, unmanageability, self-centeredness, resentments, character defects, and broken relationships. My work in the Steps includes admissions, turning things over, removing character defects, making amends, and finding humility. Even at the Tenth Step, I still find myself "wrong." So when do I see this goodness in myself? It does not show up on my Fourth Step inventory or in

---

[13] Walt Whitman, *To You.*
[14] *Twelve and Twelve*, at p. 105.
[15] *Big Book,* at p. 61.

my Fifth Step admissions. It does not form the basis for my Ninth Step amends. And it is not seeing my goodness that takes me into a Tenth Step inventory and admission. No, the goodness is not in any of that, it is not in any of the things I am directly working on in the program. The "self-searching" of Steps Four through Ten is focused on "the dark and negative side of our nature."[16]

I find the goodness in me is what is left over after the admissions are heard, the defects are removed, and the amends are made. It is "the good that is in us all" that is nurtured by prayer and meditation.[17] It is the deeper, higher part of me that was blocked out by all the personal aspects of my alcoholism, that only comes into view as I clean up the wreckage of the past through my work on the Steps. It is the gift of "a new state of consciousness and being" that the Twelfth Step speaks of. It is the transformation of the alcoholic that leaves him "in possession of a degree of honesty, tolerance, unselfishness, peace of mind, and love of which he had thought himself quite incapable."[18] And when I see that goodness in me, there is a spiritual awakening.

Rainer Maria Rilke, the great spiritual poet of the past century, captured this sense of finding the higher self – the goodness – coming out of the awareness of the desolation of self:

I am praying again, Awesome One.

You hear me again, as words
from the depths of me
rush toward you in the wind.
I've been scattered in pieces,
torn by conflict,
mocked by laughter,
washing down in drink.

---

[16] *Twelve and Twelve,* at p. 98.
[17] *Twelve and Twelve,* at p. 98.
[18] *Twelve and Twelve,* at p. 107.

The Spirituality of Sobriety

In alleyways I sweep myself up
out of garbage and broken glass.
With my half-mouth I stammer you,
who are eternal in your symmetry.
I lift to you my half-hands
in wordless beseeching, that I may find again
the eyes with which I once beheld you.

I am a house gutted by fire
where only the guilty sometimes sleep
before the punishment that devours them
hounds them out into the open.

I am a city by the sea
sinking into a toxic tide.
I am strange to myself, as though someone unknown
had poisoned my mother as she carried me.

It's here in all the pieces of my shame
that now I find myself again.
I yearn to belong to something, to be contained
in an all-embracing mind that sees me
as a single thing.
I yearn to be held
in the great hands of your heart –
oh let them take me now.
Into them I place these fragments, my life,
and you, God – spend them however you want.[19]

In stark imagery familiar to many an alcoholic, it almost seems Rilke is
describing the process of finding the higher self "in all the pieces of my

---

[19] Rainer Maria Rilke, *Book of Hours,* translated by Anita Barrows and Joanna Macy.

shame" that came out in the process of working my way through the Steps in early recovery. The finding of myself again through that kind of work is the spiritual awakening.

As I continue in recovery, I continue to get better and grow up more and more. As we say, it is progress, not perfection. But as I have accumulated some time now in recovery, I have the "opportunity" to see in my sober past those things that I have said or done which I would now do quite differently because of continued growth and development. I am not talking about the things done in my drinking past, things I think of as the consequences of my drinking and alcoholism. Rather, I am talking about things done in sobriety with some period of time already in active recovery. And I am not thinking so much here of things that are "wrong." Rather, it is things I said or did that were the best I could do at the time, but were less skillful or enlightened than what I could do today. Taking these experiences through the Steps and finding resolution for them is possible for me today because of the spiritual awakening, because of that deeper, higher self that I keep finding as the expression of God's absolute unconditional love for me. And so, the synchronicity between my continued sobriety and this spiritual awakening keeps the program working for me today.

Chapter 3
The Nature of Alcoholism

"We admitted we were powerless over alcohol –
that our lives had become unmanageable."

Step One

Alcoholism is a disease. The alcoholic seems to have some genetic predisposition to drink. There are many texts and books on the medical description of alcoholism and treatment protocols. Our own experience of the effects of long drinking has shown us that "the body of the alcoholic is quite as abnormal as his mind."[1] As part of our service work in A.A., we often assist the suffering alcoholic in obtaining hospitalization and treatment. Our literature recognizes alcoholism to be "a seemingly hopeless state of mind and body."[2] While initial hospitalization and rehabilitation for detoxification is important for the suffering alcoholic, the ultimate solution to the alcohol problem worked out in the experience of recovering alcoholics in A.A. is not found in hospitalization, treatments or physical cures. It is found "on the spiritual as well as an altruistic plane."[3]

Much has been written about the development of craving and the obsession to drink that so occupies the mind of the real alcoholic, driving her to yet another spree. It is with this obsession that the A.A. recovery program begins. Hospitalization and medical treatment may often be required to stabilize the active alcoholic, relieve his physical suffering and

---

[1] *Big Book*, at p. xxiv.
[2] *Big Book*, at pp. xiii and 20.
[3] *Big Book*, at p. xxiv.

33

clear his mind. But it is the obsession that leads this person back to the bar upon discharge from the hospital. And it is this obsession that becomes the focus of the spiritual solution. Our entire program of recovery comes into sharp focus at the point of the alcoholic's obsession to drink. "A.A.'s Twelve Steps are a group of principles, spiritual in their nature, which, if practiced as a way of life, can expel the obsession to drink and enable the sufferer to become happily and usefully whole."[4]

When I first came into recovery, I wanted to know why I drank the way I did. But when I asked people, I was told that I drank that way because I was an alcoholic. "Look, Gregg, it's your nature as an alcoholic to drink. Fish swim in water; you swim in a sea of alcohol." This answer satisfied me for some months while I sobered up and dried out, but left me wondering afterwards. There was yet another, deeper, level to the question. If I drank because I had a disease with an obsession to drink, then why did I continue to drink after I understood my condition? Now that I had stopped, why would I ever start again? And yet that is the very tragic condition of the alcoholic. Knowing her condition, "the actual or potential alcoholic, with hardly an exception, will be *absolutely unable to stop drinking on the basis of self-knowledge*."[5]

Why cannot we stop and stay stopped? The answer seems to be in the very nature of the alcoholic that distinguishes us from the non-alcoholic problem drinker – the loss of "the ability to control our drinking."[6] Our literature provides a very simple definition of the alcoholic: "If, when you honestly want to, you find you cannot quit entirely, or if when drinking, you have little control over the amount you take, you are probably alcoholic."[7] It is all about control and lack of control. My own drinking experience showed my total lack of control over my drinking, even in the face of grave consequences. Once I found a break in the wall of my denial, saw the connection between the consequences and the drinking, then the conclusion of my lack of control over my drinking was inevitable. No sane

---

[4] *Twelve and Twelve*, at p. 15.
[5] *Big Book*, at p. 39.
[6] *Big Book*, at p. 30.

[7] *Big Book*, at p. 44.

person would drink knowing the certainty and gravity of the consequences that come to the drinking alcoholic.

Given all this, I again asked myself, why do I drink the way I do? Knowing for certain that I am alcoholic, why must I continue to practice a spiritual program of recovery to prevent a return to drink? Again, it is all about the obsession. When the obsession is upon me, when I have that strong urge to drink, there is little I can do to control it at that point. I may delay the drinking, but the inevitability of a pending drunk is clear. So, the work is at a lower level: to remove the obsession itself. Now I am at the level where the Twelve Steps begin their work. This work is the lifetime practice of the Twelve Steps that can "expel the obsession to drink."[8] This is our work in recovery. This is the work that requires a power greater than ourselves to help us do what we cannot do ourselves. It is this same work that requires our willingness, honesty, and openness. And it is this work that will bring about the spiritual experience that will remove the obsession and "enable the sufferer to become happily and usefully whole."[9]

"Sometimes we hear an alcoholic say that the only thing he needs to do is to keep sober."[10] Why isn't this enough? Why isn't it sufficient to simply not drink and go to meetings? Why all the spiritual stuff, and why this insistence upon working the Steps? Because simply not drinking leaves us at the level of the problem, but not at the level of the solution. "Our liquor was but a symptom. So we had to get down to causes and conditions."[11] More is required in order to assure against a return to active alcoholism. "We feel a man is unthinking when he says that sobriety is enough."[12]

It seems our literature is encouraging me to do some thinking at this point. If I can begin to see these causes and conditions that will drive me to drink notwithstanding my knowledge of myself as an alcoholic, then the Steps and the necessity for a spiritual solution all begin to make sense. "We feel that elimination of our drinking is but a beginning. A much more important demonstration of our principles lies before us in our respective

[8] *Twelve and Twelve*, at p. 15.
[9] *Twelve and Twelve*, at p. 15.
[10] *Big Book*, at p. 82.
[11] *Big Book*, at p. 64.
[12] *Big Book*, at p. 82.

homes, occupations and affairs."[13] Not drinking is a good start for me. But the failure to take on a lifetime practice of the Twelve Steps and work out the principles of recovery in all aspects of my life is the ongoing threat to my sobriety, and my newfound happiness. "The spiritual life is not a theory. *We have to live it.*"[14]

---

[13] *Big Book*, at p. 19.
[14] *Big Book*, at p. 83.

Chapter 4
The Causes and Conditions of My Drinking

*"Our licquor was but a symptom. So we had
to get down to causes and conditions."*

Big Book

Now I am ready to take a look at those "causes and conditions" of my drinking. Again, I ask the question, why do I drink the way I do?

"We thought 'conditions' drove us to drink, and when we tried to correct these conditions and found that we couldn't to our entire satisfaction, our drinking went out of hand and we became alcoholics."[1] I can still remember hearing this sentence read from the *Twelve and Twelve* during an A.A. Step meeting after some time in recovery. I was hearing the sentence as a statement of truth, and agreeing with it. I did believe conditions outside myself were the cause of my drinking. And, I still believed that if I could just straighten out all those conditions, then I wouldn't have to drink over everything. I had not yet seen that the sentence was a set up to show how our thinking about "conditions" had been wrong.

---

[1] *Twelve and Twelve*, at p. 47.

The Spirituality of Sobriety

As the person across the room continued reading the paragraph the next sentence came right off the page at me: "It never occurred to us that we needed to change ourselves to meet conditions, whatever they were."[2] As I sat in my chair at that meeting, I had a spiritual awakening, a paradigm shift as people say in my business meetings at work today. First, I saw the impossibility of my ever succeeding in changing all the conditions around me which I blamed for my drinking. Suddenly I realized that changing those conditions was not the solution to my drinking problem. I saw how I had been trying to hold myself steady while I changed everything around me, and that the new work I needed to take on was to allow everything around me to hold steady while I sought change within myself! I needed to stop trying to change conditions to meet my demands. Instead, I needed to change my demands so that they met the conditions around me. This may seem obvious to some, but then great spiritual truths often are obvious. And this one struck me with sudden force and resulted in an immediate course correction in how I sought to live my life.

I had just received the message that my drinking was not caused by conditions outside myself. So what was the cause? The A.A. literature is quite clear about the answer and even suggests that I should have seen it as a newcomer early in sobriety. The *Twelve and Twelve* identifies two causes — a primary or underlying cause, and then an immediate cause. The literature identifies "character defects" as the primary cause of alcoholic drinking, and defective relationships with people as the immediate cause of drinking:

> By now the newcomer has probably arrived at the following conclusions: that his character defects, representing instincts gone astray, have been the primary cause of his drinking and his failure at life.[3]

---

[2] *Twelve and Twelve*, at p. 47.
[3] *Twelve and Twelve*, at p. 50.

The Causes and Conditions of My Drinking

Alcoholics especially should be able to see that instinct run wild in themselves is the underlying cause of their destructive drinking.[4]

Whatever the defects, they have finally ambushed us into alcoholism and misery.[5]

... those serious character flaws that made problem drinkers of us in the first place, flaws that must be dealt with to prevent a retreat into alcoholism once again.[6]

... defective relations with other human beings have nearly always been the immediate cause of our woes, including our alcoholism ....[7]

Now it becomes transparently clear to me why Steps Four through Seven focus on my character defects and why Steps Eight and Nine focus on my relationships. The heart of the Twelve Steps goes directly to the primary and immediate causes of my drinking. If I hope to maintain a meaningful sobriety, I am going to have to work a solution that operates at the level of these "causes and conditions" of the problem. And those causes and conditions do not arise from the situations and events of life around me. Rather, they exist inside me – my character defects and my inability to get along with the people around me.

While we may think of this as psychological work, and some may obtain great assistance from psychological counseling, the literature provides a course of recovery for us that is worked out on a spiritual plane.[8] Identifying our character defects and making amends follows the practices of confession and reconciliation found in many religious faiths and traditions. While I spend a great deal of effort inventorying and

[4] *Twelve and Twelve*, at p. 44.
[5] *Twelve and Twelve*, at p. 54.
[6] *Twelve and Twelve*, at p. 73.

[7] *Twelve and Twelve*, at p. 80.
[8] *Big Book*, at p. xxiv.

admitting my character defects, I ultimately look to my Higher Power for their removal. Similarly, the solution for defective relationships is a list of harms done and taking action to make amends. An acknowledgement of harm done and the making of a true amend may be the height of spirituality achieved by a person in her lifetime. I have certainly found the presence of my Higher Power in the healing of broken relationships.

Chapter 5
Character Defects and Instincts Run Wild

*"...character defects, representing instincts
gone astray, have been the primary cause
of his drinking and his failure at life."*

Twelve and Twelve

Since character defects, or flaws or shortcomings (as the A.A.
literature variously refers to them), are the primary cause of my
alcoholism, and since much of the spiritual program of recovery concerns
the acknowledgement and removal of them, I am going to need to really
understand what they are, how to see them, where they come from, what
they do to me, and how they can be removed. Perhaps the best place to
start is to see where they do not come from.

What I want to believe is that my character defects arise from my
drinking, and that simply stopping the drinking will result in the removal of
my character defects. However, our literature, once again, is very clear that
my beliefs and opinions about my drinking are all wrong and typically
backwards.

We shall claim that our serious character defects, if we think we
have any at all, have been *caused* chiefly by excessive drinking.
This being so, we think it logically follows that sobriety – first,
last, and all the time – is the only thing we need to work for. We
believe that our one-time good characters will be revived the

The Spirituality of Sobriety

moment we quit alcohol. If we were pretty nice people all along, except for our drinking, what need is there for a moral inventory now that we are sober?[1]

Just as I was wrong about the causes of my drinking, I have also confused the causes with the results of my drinking. Character defects are a cause of my drinking, not a result of my drinking. Ceasing drinking alone does not remove my character defects, because drinking is not the cause of my defects. The reason why it is so very important to see this relationship is because the corollary is also true – if I do not seek the removal of my character defects, it is not likely that I will be able to remain sober. Those "serious character flaws" that were responsible for our alcoholism "must be dealt with to prevent a retreat into alcoholism once again."[2]

But, we get ahead of the story here. Removal of defects forms the heart of the Steps, at Six and Seven. The point here is simply that these defects are not caused by my drinking. So how are they caused? What are character defects, and where do they come from?

Those coming from a religious training may think of these character defects as "serious violations of moral principles," while others may think of them as personality defects or "an index of maladjustments."[3] The *Twelve and Twelve* suggests using the Seven Deadly Sins as "a universally recognized list" of these defects: pride, greed, lust, anger, gluttony, envy, and sloth.[4] While these defects seem clear in their primary colors, the literature recognizes a shading or gradation of them away from the extremes to "less violent aspects of these very same defects," with perhaps a "milder" word for the less extreme form of the defect.[5]

So now we have names for the various character defects, but that still does not answer where they come from and what causes them to arise. Are they simply man's moral depravity or original sin? The literature finds a

---

[1] *Twelve and Twelve*, at p. 45.
[2] *Twelve and Twelve*, at p. 73.
[3] *Twelve and Twelve*, at p. 48

[4] *Twelve and Twelve*, at p. 48.
[5] *Twelve and Twelve*, at pp. 66-67.

Character Defects and Instincts Run Wild

much less judgmental explanation for the source of our character defects. The *Twelve and Twelve* defines character defects simply as "instincts gone astray."[6] Now in order to understand the origin of our character defects, we must first understand what instincts are according to the literature.

The literature expressly identifies three basic instincts common to all people: "for the sex relation, for material and emotional security, and for companionship," or more succinctly, "sex, security, and society."[7] Nothing in any way evil is attributed to these instincts. Rather, the literature recognizes that they "are perfectly necessary and right, and surely God-given," and are simply part of how we were created and an essential part of human beings.[8] They are given to man by God to "help him stay alive."[9] The problems only arise as our instincts begin to exceed their normal bounds:

> Yet these instincts, so necessary for our existence, often far exceed their proper functions. Powerfully, blindly, many times subtly, they drive us, dominate us, and insist upon ruling our lives. Our desires for sex, for material and emotional security, and for an important place in society often tyrannize us. When thus out of joint, man's natural desires cause him great trouble, practically all the trouble there is.[10]

As these God-given instincts begin to exceed their bounds, they begin to cause trouble for all people. In the alcoholic, these instincts "run wild," far exceeding their proper function.[11] The extent to which we permit these instincts to drive our thinking and behavior beyond their normal bounds becomes "the measure of our character defects:"

> Since most of us are born with an abundance of natural desires, it isn't strange that we often let these far exceed their intended purpose. When they drive us blindly, or we willfully demand that

---

[6] *Twelve and Twelve*, at p. 50.
[7] *Twelve and Twelve*, at pp. 42 and 49.
[8] *Twelve and Twelve*, at p. 42.
[9] *Twelve and Twelve*, at p. 64.
[10] *Twelve and Twelve*, at p. 42.
[11] *Twelve and Twelve*, at p. 44

they supply us with more satisfactions or pleasures than are possible or due us, that is the point at which we depart from the degree of perfection that God wishes for us here on earth. That is the measure of our character defects....[12]

So these character defects are simply the result of natural, God-given instincts running beyond their normal bounds, tyrannizing us and running our lives.

But, we may ask, how does that happen? If I let my instincts run wild, why don't I simply end up with an abundance of satisfaction of my instinctual desires? It seems that would be a good thing, since God gave me these instincts and they are "perfectly necessary and right."[13] Unfortunately, when the instincts run past their normal bounds, the result is something other than simply an excess of satisfaction of the desire. Our literature specifically identifies several things that result:

Unhappiness – "Every time a person imposes his instincts unreasonably upon others, unhappiness follows."[14]

Trouble – "When thus out of joint, man's natural desires cause him great trouble."[15]

Conflict – "This collision of instincts can produce anything from a cold snub to a blazing revolution. In these ways we are set in conflict not only with ourselves, but with other people who have instincts, too."[16]

No Peace – "Whenever a human being becomes a battleground for the instincts, there can be no peace."[17]

---

[12] *Twelve and Twelve*, at p. 65.
[13] *Twelve and Twelve*, at p. 42.
[14] *Twelve and Twelve*, at p. 44.

[15] *Twelve and Twelve*, at p. 42.
[16] *Twelve and Twelve*, at p. 44.
[17] *Twelve and Twelve*, at p. 44.

Character Defects and Instincts Run Wild

Emotional Problems – "Nearly every serious emotional problem can be seen as a case of misdirected instinct."[18]

Physical and Mental Problems – "When that happens, our great natural assets, the instincts, have turned into physical and mental liabilities."[19]

And, as a final result for alcoholics, we "see that instinct run wild in themselves is the underlying cause of their destructive drinking."[20]

As those "perfectly necessary and right" natural instincts become incessant demands for more and more satisfaction, fear that we may not obtain the satisfaction of those desires arises. For example, if the normal bound for satisfaction of the instinctual need for financial security is $100, and if the measure of my character defect in this regard is ten times the normal bound, then I am trying to obtain $1,000. My incessant demand for more and more above the normal $100 is likely to cause others to resist me. As others achieve their $100 goal, but I continue to direct all my efforts toward achieving my $1,000 goal, I am quite likely to develop a fear of not reaching the $1,000 as I encounter difficulties and setbacks. Of course, I may have long ago exceeded the normal bound of $100 that works for everyone else. But I continue to believe I must have more. My fear of not achieving the $1,000, especially after I have exceeded the $100, is seen by others as an unreasonable fear. This example dealing with financial security is easy — working with numbers — but the same principle applies to emotional security, as well as our instinctual needs for sex and society.

Then this unreasonable fear itself gives rise to the various character defects as I continue to demand greater satisfaction of needs notwithstanding my failure and the resistance of others to my demands.

---

[18] *Twelve and Twelve*, at p. 42.
[19] *Twelve and Twelve*, at p. 42.
[20] *Twelve and Twelve*, at p. 44.

The Spirituality of Sobriety

Unreasonable fear that our instincts will not be satisfied drives us to *covet* the possessions of others, to *lust* for sex and power, to become *angry* when our instinctive demands are threatened, to be *envious* when the ambitions of others seem to be realized while ours are not. We eat, drink, and grab for more of everything than we need, fearing we shall never have enough.[21]

If my demand for satisfaction of an instinctual need did not exceed the normal bounds, then I would not have this unreasonable fear of never achieving satisfaction of the desire. If I were not afraid of not being able to obtain all the possessions I felt I needed, then greed would not become such an issue for me and I would not find myself coveting the possessions of others. "The chief activator of our defects has been self-centered fear – primarily fear that we would lose something we already possessed or would fail to get something we demanded."[22] In other words, the fear that our inflated needs will not be met causes us to press so hard in that area that we create a flaw or defect in our character as a result.

The character defects themselves can then spin the cycle some more, giving rise to greater demands for satisfaction of the already "out of joint" natural desires:

Pride lures us into making demands upon ourselves or upon others which cannot be met without perverting or misusing our God-given instincts. When the satisfaction of our instincts for sex, security, and society becomes the sole object of our lives, then pride steps in to justify our excesses.[23]

And so we see the progression outlined in our literature: 1) God-given natural instincts for sex, security and society; 2) the pursuit of the satisfaction of these instincts beyond their normal bounds; 3) the

---

[21] *Twelve and Twelve*, at p. 49 (emphasis added).
[22] *Twelve and Twelve*, at p. 76.
[23] *Twelve and Twelve*, at p. 49.

Character Defects and Instincts Run Wild

satisfaction of instincts becoming the sole purpose of life; 4) the inevitable results of resistance, failure, conflict and unhappiness; 5) fear that the instinctive needs will not be met; and 6) additional character defects arising from our efforts to achieve greater satisfaction of the instincts and to justify the further satisfaction of the "out of joint" instincts. For the alcoholic, this progression leads to the onset of destructive drinking. It did for me.

Chapter 6
Inventory and Admissions

"Made a searching and fearless moral inventory of ourselves."

Step Four

"Admitted to God, to ourselves, and to another human being the exact nature of our wrongs."

Step Five

Now I begin to understand why the Steps talk so little about alcohol and drinking. These are not my basic problem; rather, they are only the symptoms. Treating the symptom is not going to solve my problem. Having identified character defects as the primary cause of my drinking, the Steps now direct me to the beginning of a path leading to a solution for my basic problem – "a searching and fearless moral inventory of ourselves."

The discussion of the inventory in the Fourth Step of the *Twelve and Twelve* begins with "a closer look at what the basic problem is."[1] This "look" includes a long discussion of our difficulty with the instincts and the resulting development of character defects leading, for the alcoholic, to destructive drinking. Next, the *Twelve and Twelve* directs our attention to the inventory process itself. I would have thought that the inventory would be a listing of my character defects under the headings of the Seven Deadly

---

[1] *Twelve and Twelve*, at p. 43.

The Spirituality of Sobriety

Sins, and then a narrative of the specific instances where I had acted out each of these defects in my past life. But that is not the format suggested by the *Twelve and Twelve*. Rather, it is suggested that the alcoholic "make a rough survey of his conduct with respect to his primary instincts for sex, security, and society."[2] Questions that might be asked in relation to each of these instincts are posed. Honest answers to them will reveal the specific character defects which have arisen in the individual alcoholic. So, instead of naming the defect, and then looking for an example of it in my life, I lay out my past life in the form of answers to questions directed to my pursuit of the satisfaction of my instincts, and I allow the particular character defects to simply arise from my personal story as it unfolds in my answers.

This is why the Fourth Step inventory "is but the beginning of a lifetime practice."[3] I can always come back to this Step throughout my life because I continue to deal with these primary instincts for sex, security and society throughout my life. Hopefully, I become more skillful over time in my pursuit of the satisfaction of these instincts (more on this in the Twelfth Step as we "practice these principles in all our affairs"). But I do find myself periodically taking some time to prepare an inventory of my current conduct in regard to these instincts. This inventory then shows me what further work needs to be done in light of my continuing growth and experience.

The *Big Book* takes a little different approach to the inventory process, one that I found particularly useful early in recovery. This approach begins the search for "the flaws in our make-up" by looking at resentments and writing them down on a "grudge list."[4] While the resentments themselves must be dealt with in order to remain sober, the identification of wrongs done to us is not the end of the inventory process. It is only the beginning. The next step turns the focus of attention from the wrongs of others to a resolute looking "for our own mistakes."[5] The resentment serves as an easily observable signpost indicating where our problems are located. The

---

[2] *Twelve and Twelve*, at p. 50.
[3] *Twelve and Twelve*, at p. 50.
[4] *Big Book*, at p. 64-5.
[5] *Big Book*, at p. 67.

people, places, and things against which I hold resentments are the very places I need to be looking to find my flaws. When I am able to see past the wrongs of others and begin to see my own fault, I write that down in my list. Next, I reviewed my fears thoroughly. "We put them on paper, even though we had no resentment in connection with them."[6] Finally, I reviewed my conduct in sexual relationships looking for selfishness, dishonesty and inconsiderateness.[7] The conclusion of the *Big Book's* inventory: "We have listed and analyzed our resentments.... We have listed the people we have hurt by our conduct, and are willing to straighten out the past if we can."[8] In this manner, I am led through a search that culminates in the identification of my character defects.

While I personally found the *Big Book's* approach most useful early in my recovery (see Chapter 7), its benefits are available any time resentments, fears, and intimacy issues arise ("We all have sex problems!"[9]). The benefit of the approach is not just the resolution of the resentment, fear, or relationship issue. Of even greater importance, these inventory items become windows providing visibility to an area of my life needing attention. They become like large neon signs flashing the directions to an area where one of my character defects, that would rather not be seen and identified, is hiding out.

Having created a written inventory of my character defects either by tracing my unreasonable pursuit of the satisfaction of the primary instincts, or by looking through the window of my personal resentments, fears and intimacy issues, I now have in front of me on paper a detailed description of the primary causes of my drinking. For the first time in my life, I have a chance to see my problem clearly. I have "swallowed and digested some big chunks of truth about [my]self."[10] Now what?

We are not expected to sit alone with our problem. It is strongly suggested that we move to the Fifth Step, making an admission of the exact nature of our wrongs to ourselves, to God, and, perhaps most importantly,

---

[6] *Big Book*, at p. 68.
[7] *Big Book*, at p. 69.
[8] *Big Book*, at p. 70.

[9] *Big Book*, at p. 69.
[10] *Big Book*, at p. 71.

The Spirituality of Sobriety

to another person. A.A. experience indicates that it is not likely we will long remain sober holding alone the tension and anxiety associated with those "big chunks of truth." Both the *Big Book* and the *Twelve and Twelve* contain express warnings of relapse if we fail to complete the Fifth Step:

> "If we skip this vital step, we may not overcome drinking....
> Almost invariably they got drunk."[11]

> "Most of us would declare that without a fearless admission of our defects to another human being we could not stay sober."[12]

At the same time, the *Twelve and Twelve* recognizes the great difficulty involved in actually talking to another person about the dark secrets of our lives which we had thought would go with us to the grave. A high degree of willingness is required. "No one ought to say the A.A. program requires no willpower; here is one place you may require all you've got."[13]

While we are speaking to God and another person about many of the things on our inventory and making an admission of the exact nature of our wrongs, this is not an admission in some legal or religious sense. In the pursuit of recovery from alcoholism and the desire to obtain long-term sobriety, we are not so directly concerned with issues of morality and religion. The emphasis in this Step is not on the necessity of making an admission because we have been found guilty of some moral infraction. Rather, I make the admission because I cannot carry by myself alone the weight of the knowledge of my shortcoming. I need to share this with another human being. "If we have swept the searchlight of Step Four back and forth over our careers, and it has revealed in stark relief those experiences we'd rather not remember..., then the need to quit living by ourselves with those tormenting ghosts of yesterday gets more urgent than ever. We have to talk to somebody about them."[14]

---

[11] *Big Book*, at pp. 72-73.
[12] *Twelve and Twelve*, at pp. 56-57.
[13] *Twelve and Twelve*, at p. 61.

Inventory and Admissions

The sharing of my secrets with another human being achieved several immediate benefits for me. First, the issues causing me problems in life came into sharp focus as I discussed them with my sponsor. The issues were no longer hidden in a fog of denial, rationalization, explanation, justification, and blame of others. Now I could see the issue more clearly and how I was the cause of my own problem. Second, the secrets were no longer hidden away inside of me waiting to arise out of my subconscious in some twisted, sideways manner and ambush me as I was otherwise going about my life. Rather, they received direct and focused attention and could now be dealt with in a conscious manner. Third, the pressure and anxiety associated with the hiding of the shortcomings was now dissipated by simply bringing it out of the confined space inside of me and into the spaciousness and light of communication between two people. Fourth, I received the indirect benefit of feeling deeply connected with another human being.

It is still a bit of a mystery to me how we, as human beings, connect at the deepest and truest level when we share our less-than-glorious moments with each other. Perhaps it is simply because we are, as humans, flawed. Connecting at the broken places gives rise to the deep sympathies and feelings of love, forgiveness, humility and gratitude. A connection at any other level remains superficial to our true humanness. Finally, I felt a much deeper sense that I now belonged in my A.A. group. I hesitate to use the word "initiation," but that is what it felt like for me. Having made my admissions to another human being, I had fully opted into the group. From my own mouth had come the words that identified me with the rest of the group. I was no longer an outsider objectively observing the group to determine if I belonged here. I was on the inside now, part of the group, with a chair at the meeting that belonged to me every week.

As I continue in the "lifetime practice" of taking inventory of my conduct in regard to my instincts for sex, security and society, I will need to

---

[14] *Twelve and Twelve*, at p. 55.

The Spirituality of Sobriety

follow up those inventories with a Fifth Step admission to God, myself, and another human being. The follow-up inventory itself remains of diminished value until I speak of my findings with another. And, having completed the inventory and brought the issue out into the open, the actual need to talk with another about it will, again, become more pressing. The *Twelve and Twelve* tells us that "scarcely any Step is more necessary to longtime sobriety and peace of mind than this one."[15]

I could not carry my problems alone when I was new into recovery, and I still cannot carry them alone after I am ten years in recovery. The point of recovery is not to develop the capability of holding our problems within ourselves and remain sober. Rather, the point is to develop the ability to share our problems with another and so remain sober. The difference between my early recovery and my later years is that I now have a capacity to simply and naturally share these things with my friends and soulmates both in and out of the A.A. community. This level of sharing has become part of my relationship with the people who are close to me. What I did early in recovery as a very formal written inventory and a specific appointment with my sponsor for the making of admissions, I now do as a regular and normal part of intimate conversation with those close to me. The things that I am "sore" about, and that "burn" me up are things that become the topic of my conversation with close friends and family. In this process, I receive feedback, suggestions, and bits of guidance from many different people as I share these things in our conversation.

I consider this intimate sharing of my problems to be important for my long-term sobriety because of the warnings in our literature in regard to the importance of the Fifth Step. I see the connection between avoiding this Step and relapse for me. So I now watch for the indicators identified in the *Twelve and Twelve* as warning signs for the movement away from continuing recovery and toward relapse.

---

[15] *Twelve and Twelve*, at p. 55.

Inventory and Admissions

Even A.A. oldtimers, sober for years, often pay dearly for skimping this Step. They will tell how they tried to carry the load alone; how much they suffered of irritability, anxiety, remorse, and depression; and how, unconsciously seeking relief, they would sometimes accuse even their best friends of the very character defects they themselves were trying to conceal.[16]

When I am feeling irritable, anxious, remorseful, or depressed, or I am blaming others, I now get a reminder that perhaps I need to look at a Fifth Step. Am I trying to carry some load alone rather than sharing the shortcoming or problem with another, and thereby gaining the relief and help immediately available to me from so simple an act? It may be that the depression or anxiety, etc., are pointing to something else, or arise from some other cause. But today, one possibility I will consider is the continuing need for a Fifth Step. I do not want to be one to "skimp" on this Step and find myself moving on the road of misery toward a relapse to drinking. Not when an alternative for relief is so readily available to keep me firmly in my recovery program and away from that drink.

The Fifth Step has a number of wonderful benefits expressly associated with it in our literature:

"The feeling that the drink problem has disappeared will often come strongly."[17]

"We begin to feel the nearness of our Creator.... [W]e begin to have a spiritual experience."[18]

"Our fears fall from us."[19]

---

[16] *Twelve and Twelve*, at p. 56.
[17] *Big Book*, at p. 75.
[18] *Big Book*, at p. 75.

55

"[W]e shall get rid of that terrible sense of isolation we've always had."[20]

"[W]e began to get the feeling that we could be forgiven, no matter what we had thought or done."[21]

"[W]e first felt truly able to forgive others, no matter how deeply we felt they had wronged us."[22]

"Another great dividend we may expect from confiding our defects to another human being is humility."[23]

"More realism and therefore more honesty about ourselves are the great gains we make under the influence of Step Five."[24]

"[I]t was during this stage of Step Five that he first actually felt the presence of God."[25]

No other Step contains such a list of specific benefits resulting from that one Step alone. I begin to lose some of my deep fears and begin to feel more secure in my sobriety. I am introduced to humility and forgiveness (more on both these topics in the following three chapters). We come to honestly know ourselves, perhaps for the first time in our lives, and come out of our sense of isolation from all other human beings.

Perhaps most significantly, the Fifth Step provides us the opportunity to experience the actual feeling of the presence of our Higher Power in our lives. It may be that our spiritual awakening makes its first appearance in our felt experience and consciousness at this Step. Some wonder why God's presence shows up in this Step since the Fifth Step is not usually identified

---

[19] *Big Book*, at p. 75.
[20] *Twelve and Twelve*, at p. 57.
[21] *Twelve and Twelve*, at p. 57-8.
[22] *Twelve and Twelve*, at p. 58.
[23] *Twelve and Twelve*, at p. 58.
[24] *Twelve and Twelve*, at p. 58.
[25] *Twelve and Twelve*, at p. 62.

as one of the "God" steps, *e.g.*, Steps Three and Eleven. However, Step Five does include making our admission directly to God, as well as another human being. And, the making of admissions to another person is itself a highly spiritual practice. "It has been validated in every century, and it characterizes the lives of all spiritually centered and truly religious people." [26] It will be quite difficult to move into spiritual awakening if we are hiding the facts of our lives from ourselves.

In making the admissions to another human being, my tension and anxiety dissipated as I was able to share my terrible burden with a compassionate, fellow sufferer. My relief grew further as I discovered from his comments that I was not so dreadfully unique as I had feared. The Fifth Step then becomes "a resting place" to catch our breath after the intense work just completed and before moving on to the higher ground of the remaining Steps. [27] It is suggested that we review our work so far to make sure we have a solid foundation before moving on. [28]

The work of the next four Steps focuses directly on character defects and harms done to others. If the real defects and harms are avoided or side-stepped in Steps Four and Five, the work of the remaining Steps will simply continue that fiction. It has been vitally important to me that I have my problems clearly identified and admitted in order to make the remaining Steps meaningful to my recovery and continued sobriety. Our "resting place" may then become the turning point where we begin moving away from the problem and towards the solution of our alcoholism.

---

[26] *Twelve and Twelve*, at p. 57.
[27] *Twelve and Twelve*, at p. 62.
[28] *Big Book*, at p. 75.

Chapter 7
Breaking Free of the Resentments

"But with the alcoholic, whose hope is the maintenance and growth of a spiritual experience, this business of resentment is infinitely grave. We found it is fatal."

Big Book

"Resentment is the 'number one' offender. It destroys more alcoholics than anything else."[1] When I read that line from the *Big Book* in my first months of sobriety, I knew where I had to put my immediate attention if I hoped to stay sober. I was angry, I was sore, and I was "burned up," just like the *Big Book* said.

But I couldn't see how to get started. I was completely distracted by the wrongs I believed others had done. "It's not my fault," I shouted, "I'm the victim here! Others are to blame!" And my blame list included the universe, work, traffic, God, dumb luck, my wife, and all the things I had to do because I had no choice. I needed to deal with the resentments toward the people in my life, but I felt I needed to clear up things with the universe and God first.

We talk in meetings about the difference between spirituality and religion: "Religion is for those afraid of going to hell; spirituality is for those who have been there." I found another difference during my work on resentments: "Religion is about God forgiving man; spirituality is about man

---

[1] *Big Book*, at p. 64.

forgiving God." I really thought the universe was against me, and that I had to stay ever vigilant and work very hard to manage my life, or else the universe, as God was running it, would drive me into the ground. Just like Job in the Bible, "I'm doing everything right, the best I can," I thought. "So how come God keeps bringing all this bad stuff into my life?" Of course, I never caught the connection between the bad stuff and my drinking.

How to forgive God? Sounds a bit presumptuous when stated so simply. But when troubles came, my response invariably was, "Why is this happening to me?" Implicit in this question was the unstated assumption that God was doing it to me. Then I would justify myself with my long list of reasons why it wasn't my fault, just like Job did. And my way out? A spiritual awakening as a result of Steps Two and Three. I became aware of a kind and loving Presence in the universe that had much bigger plans than my little gripes and complaints. I began to want to become part of what this God was doing in his big universe more than I wanted God to become part of what I was doing in my little world. The resentment simply fell away as I became part of something bigger than me. At first, this bigger universe was simply physical, mental and spiritual recovery for me, and making coffee and carrying the message for others. Later, the big universe grew, and now I speak regularly in facilities, and work with abused and neglected children in my state. As I get better, the universe I am a part of continues to grow bigger.

Back to the resentments. Turns out God was the easy part. Now I had to deal with the people in my life. How? "This was our course…," said the *Big Book* at page 66. So, I tried to follow the directions. First, "[w]e realized that the people who wronged us were perhaps spiritually sick." This statement hit my button. "Yes! That's the point," I cried out loud while reading. "They wronged me, they're sick. So why doesn't the program address them? Why is it addressed to me?" I was stuck. I couldn't get through the rest of the course laid out in the *Big Book*.

My breakthrough did not come for a while. Then, one Saturday afternoon I was sitting in a meeting I had never been to before, and have never been back to since, and we read the following passage from the *Big Book*:

> Driven by a hundred forms of fear, self-delusion, self-seeking, and self-pity, we step on the toes of our fellows and they retaliate. Sometimes they hurt us, seemingly without provocation, but we invariably find that at some time in the past we have made decisions based on self which later placed us in a position to be hurt.[2]

I heard a voice in my head challenging me, "Do you believe it? Why don't you take a look and see what you 'invariably find?'" I later did the looking, but I already knew what I was going to find. I couldn't see my part in my troubles before because I drew the timeline too close. I always started the timeline with the hurtful action of others. Now I had been challenged to stretch out the timeline, and look again. And, sure enough, when I did this, I invariably found my part in the hurt, just like the *Big Book* said I would.

And more than that. As I kept working this issue, looking for my part in my troubles, I came to the next paragraph in the *Big Book* that says, "So our troubles, we think, are basically of our own making." Again, the voice challenged me, "Do you believe it? Is it true for you?" I thought I could see it. Then I remembered the same phrase elsewhere: *"After all, our problems were of our own making. Bottles were only a symbol."*[3] I knew if I could take hold of this, it would change my life forever. Not something to feel bad about, or try to justify or rationalize to avoid taking the blame. Rather, it was a taking of responsibility for my life. I now had the power to do that which I could not do before. I knew I would be able to forgive the hurts others had done me. I would be free of resentments, and I would have a good chance at staying sober.

---

[2] *Big Book*, at p. 62.
[3] *Big Book,* at p. 103.

The Spirituality of Sobriety

Why did this resentment stuff become all about forgiveness? On some intuitive level, I knew that resentment was about my inability to forgive others. But I didn't understand it until I saw the equation: resentment is what I get left with after someone hurts me and I refuse to forgive them. Hurt – Refusal to forgive – Resentment. And when did I see this? Not until I was working the Eighth and Ninth Steps. Then I was making amends and asking others to forgive me the hurts I had caused them. When I was working on this side, I could see how the refusal to forgive gave rise to resentment. I could see that if others refused to forgive me, I would still go free because of the amends I was making, even though the others stayed bound by the resentment. This was the issue I had been working on earlier, just seen from the other side. When it was about others, in my Ninth Step, I could see it easily. When it was about me in my Fourth Step, it took divine intervention to bring revelation to see the necessity of forgiveness in order to be free of resentments!

Funny thing. Again, this was just what our literature was telling me. "But in A.A. we slowly learned that something had to be done about our vengeful resentments...."[4] It was a slow process for me, but now I was reading that I was actually right on track. The *Twelve and Twelve* continues: "To see how erratic emotions victimized us often took a long time. We could perceive them quickly in others, but only slowly in ourselves." With the wall of denial breaking down, and a sponsor relentlessly challenging my rationalizations and justifications, I did slowly begin to see that I was the cause of all my troubles, and that I needed profound change inside before I would have hope of serenity and a meaningful, permanent sobriety. The *Twelve and Twelve* continued, "Where other people were concerned, we had to drop the word 'blame' from our speech and thought." And as I dropped the blame, my issues became all about me, rather than all about someone else. Now I could work the second part of the Serenity Prayer, and seek the courage to

---

[4] *Twelve and Twelve*, at p. 47.

62

change the things in me that were the cause of my troubles, while accepting others just exactly the way they are. For the first time in my life, I was on my way to real freedom from the bondage of my resentments.

I began my experience with forgiveness by focusing on myself. I would forgive not because someone deserved to be forgiven, or because they were really sorry, or because they apologized, or because they didn't really mean to hurt me, or for any other reason. I would forgive simply because I did not want to be left with the resentment. I would forgive because I wanted to stay sober, not because of anything about the other person. In the course of my Ninth Step, I became willing to forgive so that I might be forgiven. As the *Twelve and Twelve* says, "If we are now about to ask forgiveness for ourselves, why shouldn't we start out by forgiving them, one and all?"[5] The question made sense to me, and I had no answer.

The connection between forgiving others and receiving forgiveness ourselves became crystal clear for me when I read that researchers were attempting to find out what motivates forgiveness. They collected a study sample of people who recounted something unforgivable happening to them. The researchers followed the group, interviewing them periodically and asking if they had forgiven the offense yet. As they came to points where people did report forgiving the offense, the researchers would probe to find out what had inspired the change since the last interview. The common thread through all the cases was that the person who reported forgiveness of the offense had, herself, been forgiven by someone else for an offense she had done. So with me. As I received forgiveness from others during my Ninth Step for offenses I had done, I found myself more than willing to forgive others their offenses toward me. Receiving forgiveness allowed me to forgive others.

Finally, I was able to come back to the *Big Book's* suggested "course" for mastering resentments on pages 66 and 67. The person who hurt me was, himself, spiritually sick. The issue for me now became how I might be

---

[5] *Twelve and Twelve*, at p. 78.

of help to him, not how to nurse my resentment or try to get even. As I stayed with this new attitude, I began to see the person who hurt me differently: "He's doing the best he can and, if he knew how to do better, he would." That just took all the poison out of the hurt for me. Then the voice inside me, one more time, asked, "Do you believe it? Is it true for you?" It didn't matter if it were true in some objective sense. What mattered was if it were true for me. If it was, then I would never see people in the same way again. Now, I could be abundant in my tolerance and patience toward others. I was now at Step Ten, where the *Twelve and Twelve* promises: "It will become more and more evident as we go forward that it is pointless to become angry, or to get hurt by people who, like us, are suffering from the pains of growing up."[6] With the realization that people were a bit sick themselves, and that they were doing the best they could, and my own growing tolerance, I found that I didn't take up the hurt so readily in the first place. While I was more ready than ever to forgive, I found less and less hurt that needed forgiving.

When I do pick up hurt today, I am getting pretty good at looking through the hurt as a window to my own character defects. I find again and again that my anger and hurt pride is no more than "the smoke screen under which we were hiding some of our defects while we blamed others for them."[7] Hurt today is not so much about the other person and what I think he did, as it is about me and my own character defects – another opportunity for more of that "lifetime practice" on the Fourth Step.

Finally, I am coming to see forgiveness of wrong done as a spiritual experience. As one spiritual master said, "There is no place on earth more sacred than where an ancient feud has been forgiven." I felt the wonder of receiving forgiveness for wrongs I had done as I completed my Ninth Step, and realized what a wonderful gift it is to give forgiveness to others who have hurt me. With growing tolerance, and the realization that it is pointless to be hurt by my perception of wrongs committed by others, I now see

---

[6] *Twelve and Twelve*, at p. 92.
[7] *Twelve and Twelve*, at p. 59.

forgiveness more as a spiritual gift to give to someone else when they feel they need it from me. As another spiritual text says, We forgive our brother "for what he did not do."[8] It's a gift I am happy to give.

Now I have come all the way back. If religion is about God forgiving man, and if I have become part of His bigger plan, then perhaps I forgive simply as part of what God is doing today in the world. As I stay busy on this work, I find myself quite removed from the necessity of having a drink today. And for that, I will be forever grateful.

---

[8] Foundation for Inner Peace, *A Course In Miracles* (Glen Ellen, CA: Foundation for Inner Peace, 1992), at p. 354.

Chapter 8
The Root of our Troubles

"Selfishness — self-centeredness! That,
we think, is the root of our troubles."

Big Book

"Made a decision to turn our will and our lives
over to the care of God as we understood Him."

Step Three

Throughout our inventories and admissions, we have been dealing with character defects arising from the poor manner in which we have sought satisfaction of our primary instincts for sex, security and society. These character defects and resulting defective relationships became the "causes and conditions" of our drinking. Our recovery program in Steps Four and Five is directly aimed at identifying these causes and conditions. However, there is a unifying theme underneath all the character defects exposed and identified through those Steps. It was actually back in the Third Step that we first identified this central problem — "self, manifested in various ways, was what had defeated us...."[1] The work in our inventories was simply seeing the "common manifestations" of this central problem.

---

[1] *Big Book*, at p. 64.

The Spirituality of Sobriety

"Selfishness—self-centeredness! That, we think, is the root of our troubles."[2] Here it is, in the Third Step, that I meet the true enemy to my recovery and continued sobriety – myself! I have seen the manifestations of it in my inventory, but the true underlying cause of all my troubles is myself. Our troubles are "basically of our own making," and "arise out of ourselves."[3] How does this happen? Why is it that self-will and self-centeredness become the root of our troubles?

First, when running on self-will I am my own independent energy source. I was always running at a different pace and in a different direction than others, and so was not moving in a synchronous manner with other people in my life. I always felt like I was singing in a chorus slightly off key, or I was marching in a parade at a different step and pace, or walking down a corridor where most people are going in the other direction. Things just did not move smoothly; the gears were always grinding.

Second, I am moving according to my own plan, and so I am "almost always in collision with something or somebody."[4] I was watching my foster-child playing on his new basketball team. His team was behind and he wanted very much to put some points on the board for them. He moved the ball down the court all by himself, and tried to move through the defense to get to the hoop for a shot. He ignored all his other players, and did not work with them in the play set up for the team by the coach. He had no help from his teammates because they did not know what he was doing. In fact, his own teammates were simply things in his way to the basket. And he had all five defenders to deal with all by himself. Needless to say, the play was not much of a success for him or for his team. Even though his motives were good—he wanted points for his team so they could win—he found himself in collision with his own teammates as well as his opponents.

Third, I find myself beginning to "move" other people into positions that seem appropriate to me. I know how the whole thing should go together, and so I am trying to control other people to enact what I believe

---

[2] *Big Book*, at p. 62.
[3] *Big Book*, at p. 62.
[4] *Big Book*, at p. 60.

to be the perfect setting. Then these other people begin to resist me. It may not be that they disagree with the setting I see; it may actually be the perfect thing for them. It is more likely they are resisting me simply because they do not want to be controlled by me. They recognize that I am not acting as just one other player on the team, but rather that I am trying to direct or coach the whole thing. And so they resist me, and I find myself in conflict with those around me. This resistance becomes particularly confusing for me if the setting I am pushing actually turns out to be one desired by the other people anyway.

A person I sponsor recently shared an experience with me that brought this "moving" of other people, and their resistance, into greater clarity. Working on a crisis assignment, he was on the telephone in his office gathering the required information. His boss walked quickly into his office and around his desk, physically put her hands on him and lifted him out of his chair. She pushed him out of his office and into a conference room, all the while telling him that she needs him in this meeting right now! He allowed himself to be forcibly moved from his office to the conference room, and did not react in any negative manner to this less-than-professional conduct on the part of his boss. But, when he got home, he felt as if he had lost all his integrity as a human being. His boss' lack of respect for his person was blatant. We discussed setting some appropriate boundaries with his boss in order to preserve his own personal integrity in the office.

In talking with him, I realized that I often act in a similar manner to his boss. In my own self-centeredness, I may not physically move people around, but I do it with words, logical persuasion and arguments. But whatever the means I may use, the person likely will feel the pressure and, like my sponsee, object to the lack of respect for his personal integrity if I am successful in "moving" him. No wonder people react to this self-centered moving of others no matter the means. It directly questions their own integrity as a person. To preserve their integrity, they must resist me.

The Spirituality of Sobriety

The manner in which I carry out the manipulation of others is not particularly important at this time and is not the issue. Nor is being right or wrong in some objective sense the issue. I may be "right," and still find myself in conflict with others. Nor is the manner in which I carry out my plans of any particular importance here. In other words, the Third Step is not where we are focused on moving my actions from mean and selfish to kind and generous. Rather, we are focused on the root problem that in all these things I am the director, the motivator, the planner, and I am pushing these things from my own self-will, and people are naturally resisting me. "Is he not really a self-seeker even when trying to be kind...? Is it not evident to all the rest of the players that these are the things he wants? And do not his actions make each of them wish to retaliate...?"[5] It is the expression of my self-will and self-centeredness that people around me are resisting, not the nature of my actions or my plans or arrangements themselves. The solution coming from Step Three is not to change the nature of my actions or to make better plans for others. Rather, the solution is to get out of the self-will and the self-centeredness.

So, how do I do that? I make a decision to turn my will and life over to the care of God. I get out of the business of running things, and let my Higher Power become the one with the plans and arrangements. The person working Step Three makes the realization that he has been "a victim of the delusion that he can wrest satisfaction and happiness out of this world if he only manages well."[6] He now resigns from the management position and takes his place as just another employee. I find true happiness as I simply find my place among the others in my life and move in a rhythm with them that is not of my own making. I do not set the beat, but rather begin to play my instrument to the same beat everyone else hears.

We actually started this process back in Steps One and Two with our admission of powerlessness over alcohol, and our reliance upon a Higher Power to restore us to sanity. We are now simply taking the next logical step

---

[5] *Big Book*, at p. 61.
[6] *Big Book*, at p. 61.

70

in that process. In Step One I admitted my life was unmanageable and in Step Two I found faith that my Higher Power could bring sanity to my life. Now, in Step Three, I simply turn my life and will over to this Higher Power to do the very things I have come to believe He can do. I do not pursue the Steps in this recovery program in order to learn how to manage my life. Rather, I learn through the Steps how to get out of the management business and turn the management of my life over to my Higher Power.

This process has already worked in regard to my alcoholism. I rather quickly turned my will and my life over to A.A. for relief of my "alcohol problem."[7] Step Three now requires that I turn my will and life over to some Higher Power "in all other matters."[8] My "many problems besides alcohol will not yield to a headlong assault powered by the individual alone."[9] Just as I could not solve my alcohol problem with my own willpower, I am not going to be able to solve my other problems that way either.

Why is it not sufficient to simply turn my will and life over to my Higher Power in relation to alcohol only? Why does the alcoholic need to continue turning his will and life over in relation to all his other problems? It is because many of these other problems are not going to be solved by "sheer personal determination," and they "make him desperately unhappy and threaten his new-found sobriety."[10] I must find a solution to my "many problems besides alcohol," or else I am likely to drink again.[11] While I may have achieved some relief from the feeling of craving and the obsession to drink, I may find myself right back to drinking to relieve the acute pain created by my problems if I cannot find some solution to them.[12] And then the alcoholism will take over and I will be off on another drinking binge, and again find myself facing the obsession to drink.

I have also found that until I turn my life over to God, I cannot see my true self. There is something a bit mysterious here. I first thought that turning all aspects of my life and will over to my Higher Power would make

---

[7] *Twelve and Twelve*, at p. 35.
[8] *Twelve and Twelve*, at p. 36.
[9] *Twelve and Twelve*, at p. 40.

[10] *Twelve and Twelve*, at p. 39.
[11] *Twelve and Twelve*, at p. 40
[12] *Twelve and Twelve*, at p. 39.

me "look like the hole in the doughnut."[13] However, I actually found the result to be the discovery of my more real self. Today, I think of this "deeper" self as the one underneath all the obsessions and compulsions which resulted from the take-over of my personality by my character defects. A famous Christian author wrote of this experience:

> The more we get what we call "ourselves" out of the way and let God take us over, the more truly ourselves we become…. In that sense our real selves are all waiting for us in Him. It is no good trying to "be myself" without Him. The more I resist Him and try to live on my own, the more I become dominated by my own heredity and upbringing and surroundings and natural desires. In fact, what I so proudly call "Myself" becomes merely the meeting place for trains of events which I never started and which I cannot stop. What I call "My wishes" become merely the desires thrown up by my physical organism or pumped into me by other men's thoughts or even suggested to me by devils…. Most of what I call "Me" can be very easily explained. It is when I turn to God, when I give myself up to His Personality, that I first begin to have a real personality of my own.[14]

It seems I am thoroughly distracted by the "manifestations of self" showing up as my character defects out of my self-centeredness. Before Step Three, I was at a place where I had no visibility of a true, inspired, eternal self underneath all that painful, loud, complaining and demanding "self" I had become. As I allow God to take the center of my life and will, I begin to glimpse my true self, my higher self, for the first time. Step Three becomes my first movement away from the ego-centered self constructed out of my character defects, and toward my true self that has been covered over and made dormant until now. This excavation work of removing the

---

[13] *Twelve and Twelve*, at p. 36.
[14] Walter Hooper, ed., *The Business of Heaven: Daily Readings from C.S. Lewis* (New York: Harcourt Brace Jovanovich, 1984), at pp. 312-13.

layers of self-centeredness built up over the years continues with great effort in Steps Six and Seven.

Step Three is practiced as part of the recovery program prior to the inventory- taking and admissions. While it seems easier to me to see self-centeredness as "the root of our troubles" after seeing its manifestations in the later Steps, it is important in practice to have taken Step Three first. At that point it is the "decision" that is important. We are setting a new course here, making a course correction from our previous way of life. "We thought well before taking this step making sure we were ready...."[15] It becomes a statement of intention to the universe about the entire direction of the remainder of our lives. As such, the *Big Book* suggests a prayer format to use for the actual taking of the Step:

> God, I offer myself to Thee—to build with me and to do with me as thou wilt. Relieve me of the bondage of self, that I may better do thy will. Take away my difficulties, that victory over them may bear witness to those I would help of Thy Power, Thy Love, and Thy Way of life. May I do Thy will always!

While the recitation of this prayer is "only a beginning," its effect will be immediate and noticeable.[16] As a statement of intention concerning the future direction of our lives, this prayer is of critical importance.

Step Three carries a special and unique weight in the Twelve Step program of recovery. It shares with Steps Four and Five the express warning that our failure to take the particular Step will quite likely become the cause of relapse taking us back to drinking.

Third Step – "Above everything, we alcoholics must be rid of this selfishness. We must, or it kills us!"[17]

---

[15] *Big Book*, at p. 63.
[16] *Big Book*, at p. 63.
[17] *Big Book*, at p. 62.

The Spirituality of Sobriety

Fourth Step – "…unless he is now willing to work hard at the elimination of the worst of these defects, both sobriety and peace of mind will still elude him."[18]

Fourth Step – "But with the alcoholic … this business of resentment is infinitely grave…. The insanity of alcohol returns and we drink again."[19]

Fifth Step – "Few muddled attitudes have caused us more trouble than holding back on Step Five. Some people are unable to stay sober at all; others will relapse periodically until they really clean house."[20]

Fifth Step – "Most of us would declare that without a fearless admission of our defects to another human being we could not stay sober."[21]

While I have found all Twelve Steps to be of great importance to my initial recovery and to my long-term sobriety, I have always paid particular attention to these three Steps because of the specific warnings concerning relapse.

Step Three is unique in the Twelve Steps. It forms the basis for the remainder of the program. We are cautioned in the *Twelve and Twelve* that "other Steps of the A.A. program can be practiced with success only when Step Three is given a determined and persistent trial."[22] In other words, I may fail in my attempt at an inventory or the making of admissions or amends, not because of difficulty with Step Four, Five, Eight, or Nine, but because I failed to take Step Three. Even if I achieve some success with the other Steps, I will find that "the effectiveness of the whole A.A. program will rest upon how well and earnestly we have tried to come to 'a decision to turn our will and our lives over to the care of God *as we understood*

---

[18] *Twelve and Twelve*, at p. 50.
[19] *Twelve and Twelve*, at p. 66.
[20] *Twelve and Twelve*, at p. 56.

[21] *Twelve and Twelve*, at pp. 56-7.
[22] *Twelve and Twelve*, at p. 40.

Him'."[23] I have come to believe that one reason for the direct relationship between Step Three and all other Steps is that all the Steps "ask us to go contrary to our natural desires…they all deflate our egos."[24] If I remain "ego-centric," then I am going to find it quite impossible to take on the work of the Twelve Steps which require a deflation of this ego.[25] Step Three is the ultimate ego deflation! This is where I flatten out that ego by taking the controls away from it and removing from it the responsibility of managing my life affairs. I am turning all this over to my Higher Power instead. Now I am positioned to effectively carry out the other Steps of my recovery program.

While we are not likely to achieve our spiritual awakening if we do not honestly appraise, admit, remove and make amends for our character defects, we do make significant progress by the setting of an intention in our Third Step prayer. Basically, at this point, everything changes. We are headed in a new direction from this point forward. While the statement of belief in Step Two was important, "faith alone can avail nothing."[26] At Step Three we engage our will to "conform with God's," perhaps for the first time in our lives.[27] The action Steps following Step Three carry out this intent in a very direct and focused manner to move us from this statement of intention to a spiritual awakening in Step Twelve.

---

[23] *Twelve and Twelve*, at pp. 34-5.
[24] *Twelve and Twelve*, at p. 55.
[25] *Big Book*, at p. 61.

[26] *Twelve and Twelve*, at p. 34.
[27] *Twelve and Twelve*, at p. 40.

Chapter 9
The Subtle Practice of Removing Character Defects

"Were entirely ready of have God remove all these defects of character."

Step Six

"Humbly asked Him to remove our shortcomings."

Step Seven

From that "resting place" at the completion of Step Five, we are invited to review our progress so far. We are now convinced of our own individual powerlessness over alcohol and have found a Higher Power who can help. We have seen our own self-centeredness as the "root of our troubles" and have stated an intention to move out of this self-centeredness by turning over our lives and wills to the care of this Higher Power. We have identified the "manifestations of self" as our character defects and now understand these defects to be the primary cause of our drinking. We have made an admission of these character defects to another human being and now find ourselves at Step Six: "Were entirely ready to have God remove all these defects of character."

How do we work this Step? It is stated in a passive tense. In my experience, when I have been thorough in my inventory ("searching and

The Spirituality of Sobriety

fearless"), and have made a complete admission to someone, then I find myself "entirely ready" to get rid of my "worst character defects" that led to my most embarrassing moments.[1] I knew I had to do something about these glaring defects right away. These are the character defects I had the most difficulty talking about in my admissions, the things I thought perhaps I could get away with not bringing up, the things that caused the most shame. There is a layer of "serious character flaws ... which must be dealt with to prevent a retreat into alcoholism once again."[2] Paradoxically, these are the defects that do not require much spiritual effort to avoid.[3]

The more difficult areas are the "less violent aspects of these very same defects."[4] Here, I am apt to continue to justify, rationalize, or deny the defects and try to avoid dealing with them. Some of them I may still enjoy, and not want to have removed yet. And here is the work involved in Step Six. It is the change of my attitude from wanting to keep *any* of my character defects to wanting them *all* removed. This is deep heart work, spiritual transformation at the place where soul and personality meet. It is an alchemy process of changing base materials of character defects into a precious and rare spiritual commodity. So, how does Step Six work on *all* my character defects?

First, I find it important to recognize that it is only character defects that are to be removed; not those basic, primary instincts for sex, security and society. "It is nowhere evident, at least in this life, that our Creator expects us fully to eliminate our instinctual drives."[5] We are going to continue with these instinctual needs for the rest of our lives, and we are going to learn a new way of dealing with them in the Twelfth Step. For now, the focus remains on the character defects – those areas where we have demanded, or been driven to seek, "more satisfactions or pleasures than are possible or due us."[6]

Second, this Step is not about my doing anything, or asking for anything (we will do our asking in Step Seven). Rather, it is about my

[1] *Twelve and Twelve*, at p. 69.
[2] *Twelve and Twelve*, at p. 73.
[3] *Twelve and Twelve*, at p. 66.

[4] *Twelve and Twelve*, at p. 66.
[5] *Twelve and Twelve*, at p. 65.
[6] *Twelve and Twelve*, at p. 65.

The Subtle Practice of Removing Character Defects

attitude toward my character defects. Step Six is "A.A.'s way of stating the best possible *attitude* one can take in order to make a beginning."[7] This is the place where I begin to let go of my strong attachment to those defects that I still cherish. I stop defending, rationalizing, and justifying my continued practice of these defects. As they arise in my life, my attitude towards them changes from defending them to detesting them and letting them go.

The *Big Book* only provides one short paragraph on Step Six, but quickly comes to the heart of the issue: "If we still cling to something we will not let go, we ask God to help us be willing."[8] It is that "clinging" that is the subject of the work in this Step. I work to extend the attitude of willingness from merely those "serious character flaws ... which must be dealt with to prevent a retreat into alcoholism once again," to include *all* my character defects in even their mildest form.[9] And that is why Step Six spends some time identifying and discussing these "less violent aspects" of our character defects.[10] We are taken methodically through all the character defects categorized as the Seven Deadly Sins from Step Four to now see those more subtle variations of the same defect.[11] Of course, we may never achieve such perfection as the actual removal of all these defects in their most subtle forms, but we are only speaking of an attitude at Step Six. Extending the attitude to all my defects states a goal, not a requirement for perfection.[12]

Third, in accordance with our new goal, we recognize that the removal of our character defects is a "lifetime job."[13] This is not something that happens immediately. Whereas many alcoholics find that the obsession to drink is lifted out of them immediately, our other defects require "patient improvement."[14] I certainly am not going to be able to spot every single defect of character during my first inventory. As I continue to grow, new

---

[7] *Twelve and Twelve*, at p. 65 (emphasis added).
[8] *Big Book*, at p. 76.
[9] *Twelve and Twelve*, at p. 73.
[10] *Twelve and Twelve*, at pp. 66ff.

[11] *Twelve and Twelve*, at p. 48.
[12] *Twelve and Twelve*, at p. 68.
[13] *Twelve and Twelve*, at p. 65.
[14] *Twelve and Twelve*, at p. 65.

areas will come into view for me. I will gain new visibility into those less violent aspects of already identified character defects. Until I see them, I cannot do the work to change my attitude toward them and ask for their removal. As these less violent aspects of character defects come up during the course of my life, I work the adjustment in my attitude toward them through the continued practice of Step Six.

And this leads directly to the final point: "Having been granted a perfect release from alcoholism, why then shouldn't we be able to achieve by the same means a perfect release from every other difficulty or defect?"[15] In short, the answer is that alcoholism is different from our character defects. Where alcoholism leads to self-destruction and so runs contrary to our own "deepest instincts," our other difficulties and defects are consistent with our instincts, just taken to an extreme. Accordingly, the solution for each is different. For the obsession to drink, God provides the opportunity for an immediate release; for our other defects, it may take some time to make progress. So, our attitude is not one of expecting an immediate removal of all our defects, but rather a simple willingness to have them so removed. However, in actual practice, "we shall have to be content with patient improvement."[16]

Perhaps most important, we come to understand from Step Six that God is not going to remove all our character defects from us. We are not going to be rendered perfect human beings simply by asking God to change us. While we, as alcoholics who have had the obsession to drink removed from us, have found that God certainly can remove defects of character, we also find in Step Six that He is not going to remove all our other defects of character in the same way. We are going to have to work toward this change ourselves, and be content with progress over time.[17]

Woops! What about the Seventh Step, where we: "Humbly asked Him to remove our shortcomings?" If we conclude from the Sixth Step that God is not going to remove all these defects, then why do we ask Him to do so in

---

[15] *Twelve and Twelve*, at p. 64.
[16] *Twelve and Twelve*, at p. 65.
[17] *Twelve and Twelve*, at pp. 63 and 65.

the very next Step? Some have found difficulty at this point, thinking their faith is questioned or weakened. They ask God to remove a defect, and it is still there tomorrow. If the work at this point is seen in this context, then the person may find himself trying to resolve character defects in the context of Step Two ("Came to believe…") instead of Steps Six and Seven. However, there is only a conflict here if we think of Steps Six and Seven as being about the actual removal of all our character defects. Actually, Step Six is the development of a new attitude toward our defects, not their actual removal. Similarly, Step Seven is not about the actual removal of our defects. Rather, this Step "concerns itself with humility."[18] The word "humility" shows up 26 times in the *Twelve and Twelve's* chapter on Step Seven. "The whole emphasis of Step Seven is on humility."[19] If we are focused on an assumption that our defects are really going away simply by our asking God to take them, then we have missed the whole point of Step Seven – we have failed to see the focus on humility.

Step Seven invites us to consider humility. I find it helpful to go back to the definition of humility provided in Step Five: "a clear recognition of what and who we really are, followed by a sincere attempt to become what we could be."[20] In other words, as I read the definition, humility becomes a simple statement of the work I have been doing in Steps Four and Five ("a clear recognition of what and who we really are"), and the work I am now undertaking in Steps Six and Seven ("a sincere attempt to become what we could be"). Seen in this light, humility is not the negative we may first impute to the word. It is simply a statement of the work we have undertaken in recovery. So, we have already encountered humility in the course of our work, and seen that it is something we must have in order to succeed in recovery. Step Seven becomes the "great turning point in our lives" where "we sought for humility as something we really wanted, rather than as something we *must* have."[21] Step Seven is not where we are first introduced to humility, but rather where our perception of humility

---

[18] *Twelve and Twelve*, at p. 70.
[19] *Twelve and Twelve*, at p. 76.
[20] *Twelve and Twelve*, at p. 58.
[21] *Twelve and Twelve*, at p. 75.

changes to something we desire and are willing to pursue for its own sake. And, once again, we find that the work of this Step is not accomplished easily and quickly. Rather, this change in our perception of humility in Step Seven is "unbelievably painful," and "takes most of us a long, long, time."[22] Obviously, there is more to this Step than a simple request to God to remove our shortcomings.

So, how do we go about getting all this humility? If we stay conscious and aware of our present situation at Step Seven, it will happen almost magically. I think of it as a kind of alchemy – changing a base metal into gold. In our case, it is changing our character defects into humility. Thomas Merton, a Trappist monk and author of many spiritual works, once said:

> This is the terrible thing about humility: that it is never fully successful. If it were only possible to be completely humble on this earth....
> But our humility consists in being proud and knowing all about it, and being crushed by the unbearable weight of it, and to be able to do so little about it.[23]

Our humility will arise out of the work we have done in our inventory and admissions. We were reminded in Step Five of the great necessity of sharing with another human being the discoveries we have made about ourselves in our inventories, and that the failure to do so will result in such pressures within us that relapse is likely. If we continue to maintain consciousness of these character defects – not fall back into denial, justification and rationalization – and maintain the willingness to have them removed, then ask for their removal, we will find humility growing in us right in the very presence of the defects themselves. It is as if the defects are transformed by the heat and pressure within us into this wonderful new thing: humility.

---

[22] *Twelve and Twelve*, at pp. 72 and 73.
[23] Thomas Merton, *Thoughts in Solitude* (New York: Noonday Press, 1958), at p. 66.

The Subtle Practice of Removing Character Defects

Truly, the Seventh Step is not about removing defects; it is about the obtaining of greater degrees of humility in the very presence of our character defects. But this is not yet the end of the work in this Step. As we grow in humility, "the most profound result of all was the change in our attitude toward God."[24] Our attitude changes from being the one making decisions and doing things with occasional help from God as we deem we need it, to a deeper continuation of that Third Step work of decreasing the ego and increasing the place of our Higher Power in our lives. We move away from "a self-determined objective" toward "the perfect objective which is of God."[25] We slowly change our perspective from being an independent entity in the universe trying to arrange things to our own benefit, to being simply just another part of the wholeness of creation. God becomes more while "I" become less. As John the Baptist, with great insight, proclaimed of the Christ, "He must increase, but I must decrease."[26] We are finally getting some degree of relief and freedom from the ego-centered life we have been living for so long. Other people, and God, begin to become more important to me than my own self-centered obsessions and compulsions that have made up my character defects. "The Seventh Step is where we make the change in our attitude which permits us, with humility as our guide, to move out from ourselves toward others and toward God."[27]

This humility, arising from our own powerlessness in the presence of our character defects, goes to the heart of our difficulties. The humility does not take on individual character defects directly. Rather, it works on the self-centeredness that we identified in Step Three as the "root of our troubles." After all, the character defects are only the "manifestations of self." Another definition of humility contained in our literature provides: "Perfect humility would be a state of complete freedom from myself, freedom from all the claims that my defects of character now lay so heavily upon me. Perfect humility would be a full willingness, in all times and

---

[24] *Twelve and Twelve,* at p. 75.
[25] *Twelve and Twelve,* at p. 68.
[26] *The Bible,* John 3:30.

[27] *Twelve and Twelve,* at p. 76.

places, to find and do the will of God."[28] Humility goes to work on the root. The manifestations are thereby all affected, albeit indirectly.

This developing connection between the Third and Seventh Steps is deeply reflected in the *Big Book*. Both these Steps are directed toward God, one by way of a decision and one by a direct request. Other than the discussion of the St. Francis prayer in Step Eleven in the *Twelve and Twelve*, the Third and Seventh Steps are the only ones for which we are provided a specific prayer. It may be interesting to note that the prayer is itself the only thing the *Big Book* gives us on the Seventh Step. The two prayers themselves reveal a continuing development along a continuum. In the Third Step prayer, we open with: "God, I offer myself to Thee – to build with me and to do with me as Thou wilt."[29] We then find the same offering in the opening of the Seventh Step prayer, just at a deeper level: "My Creator, I am now willing that you should have all of me, good and bad."[30] Moreover, the prayer shows that I am not maintaining an independent status from God and then asking Him to take something from me. Rather, I am giving myself to Him – the good stuff and the character defects. He gets the whole person at this Step.

Why don't we work on the character defects directly? Some we may. Remember, "those serious character flaws" that threaten us with relapse must be dealt with directly and quickly. Where I see the alchemical changing of defects into humility by continuing consciousness of the defect itself is with all those other defects, often of a less violent nature, that I still enjoy and find more difficult to give up. As we found in Step Six, removing the more extreme defects does not require much spiritual effort. Removing the rest of the defects will require this kind of effort. After all, these are the defects that become my obsessions and compulsions. These defects I may continue to live with for a long time. But, as I keep them in full awareness, as I see myself acting them out in real life situations, as I let that pressure and heat build without relieving the pressure by further acting out the

---

[28] *The Best of Bill* (New York: AA Grapevine, 1990), at pp. 49-50.
[29] *Big Book*, at p. 63.
[30] *Big Book*, at p. 76.

The Subtle Practice of Removing Character Defects

defect, as I continue with my new attitude of desiring its removal and continue with my humble request for its removal, something mysterious happens in the cauldron of my heart. Where I had only seen the defect before, I begin to see something new, something rare and precious – the humility that had long evaded me.

Rumi has a wonderful story showing the change in attitude of the one in the boiling cauldron being transformed into something new and delicious:

A chickpea leaps almost over the rim of the pot
where it's being boiled.

"Why are you doing this to me?"

The cook knocks him down with the ladle.

"Don't you try to jump out.
You think I'm torturing you.
I'm giving you flavor,
so you can mix with spices and rice
and be the lovely vitality of a human being....

Eventually the chickpea
will say to the cook,
          "Boil me some more.
Hit me with the skimming spoon.
I can't do this by myself...."[31]

With time in the cauldron, our attitude changes as we come to understand the profound change happening within us as the work of Steps Six and

---

[31] Coleman Barks, tr., *The Essential Rumi* (New York: HarperCollins, 1995) , at pp. 132-133.

The Spirituality of Sobriety

Seven continues through the years. This is the "great turning point in our lives ... when we sought for humility as something we really wanted, rather than as something we *must* have."[32]

I find it interesting that those outside recovery face the same issues in dealing with their character defects as part of a spiritual practice leading to a contemplative state. Thomas Merton divides faults into two groups, similar to the Seventh Step:

> However, it is relatively simple to get rid of faults that we recognize as faults – although that too can be terribly hard. But the crucial problem of perfection and interior purity is in the renunciation and uprooting of all our *unconscious* attachments to created things and to our own will and desires.[33]

Merton provides some detail for dealing with the first group. The goal is to develop a good habit in lieu of the fault. The work is by way of resolutions, giving things up, hanging on and resisting. But Merton recognizes that with the second group, what he calls "the deep and unconscious habits of attachment which we can hardly dig up and recognize," all these kinds of efforts on our part are ineffective:

> In getting the best of our secret attachments – ones which we cannot see because they are principles of spiritual blindness – our own initiative is almost always useless. We need to leave the initiative in the hands of God working in our souls either directly in the night of aridity and suffering, or through events and other men.[34]

And then Merton arrives at the same conclusion concerning these less violent aspects of our character defects and our inability to remove them directly as we did in the Seventh Step: "we may be left with faults we cannot

[32] *Twelve and Twelve*, at p. 75.
[33] Thomas Merton, *New Seeds of Contemplation* (New York: New Directions, 1961), at p. 256.
[34] *New Seeds of Contemplation,* at p. 257.

The Subtle Practice of Removing Character Defects

conquer – in order that we may have the *humility* to fight against a seemingly unbeatable opponent, without any satisfaction of victory."[35] Just like the Seventh Step, Merton finds this process of dealing with the more unconscious faults to really be a process for the development of humility in us.

Sufism may even take this thinking another step farther with its concept of the need to integrate the shadow part of ourselves with our more conscious awareness. "In fact, if you want to know what your qualities are, all you have to do is ask yourself what your defects are – because you have the qualities of which your defects are the shadow."[36]

Rumi provides a more positive perspective on this process of waiting upon our Higher Power to remove our character defects:

> An empty mirror and your worst destructive habits,
> when they are held up to each other,
> that's when the real making begins.
> That's what art and crafting are.
>
> A tailor needs a torn garment to practice his expertise.
> The trunks of trees must be cut and cut again
> so they can be used for fine carpentry.
>
> Your doctor must have a broken leg to doctor.
> Your defects are the ways that glory gets manifested.[37]

It is God's work to make art out of our defects, so He needs defects as His raw material for His "art and crafting."

---

[35] Thomas Merton, *Thoughts in Solitude* (New York: Noonday Press, 1958), at p. 31 (emphasis added).

[36] Pir Vilayat Inayat Khan, *That Which Transpires Behind That Which Appears* (New Lebanon, NY: Omega Publications, 1994), at p. 116.

[37] *The Book of Love,* at p. 138.

The Spirituality of Sobriety

So, what becomes of these more subtle character defects? Over time, they become less of a feature in our lives. The reason these character defects begin to show up less in our lives is simple – they are simply not activated in the presence of our new-found humility. "The chief activator of our defects has been self-centered fear – primarily fear that we would lose something we already possessed or would fail to get something we demanded."[38] I read this sentence for years focusing on the fear aspect. And that is important. But it is more important to realize I am dealing with a particular kind of fear as the activator of my defects. For example, walking up on a grizzly bear while hiking in the woods is going to cause fear for me. But it may not be self-centered. Rather, the first thought I may have is likely to be about my children with me and their protection. And this fear may activate self-sacrificing energies within me to save my children. Fear, itself, is not necessarily the activator of my defects. But the self-centered kind of fear described above does become the activator of my defects as I try to assure I get or keep what I want. It is this "whole lifetime geared to self-centeredness" that the humility gained in Step Seven works against.[39]

As we grow more in this humility, there is less self-centered fear, and so our defects are not activated so much. That is why they begin to show up less and less in our lives over time. It is like the movie, *A Beautiful Mind*, in which the Nobel prize winning mathematician suffering from schizophrenia continues to see his hallucinations while struggling against them. Although the hallucinations still try to gain his attention, they show up in his life at greater distances from him, and finally just wave to him rather hopelessly. I often picture my defects as small cog wheels in a watch trying to engage the large wheel in the middle. As long as I do not engage the cogs of my large wheel with the cogs of the character defect spinning wildly around, it will not be able to put me into a spin and I will not act out the defect. It is like the "magic moment" therapists sometimes talk about

---

[38] *Twelve and Twelve*, at p. 76.
[39] *Twelve and Twelve*, at p. 73.

The Subtle Practice of Removing Character Defects

where we have a quarter-second to choose whether to act on a feeling. After that, hormones and physical reactions have already started, making it much more difficult not to act out the emotion. So now, in addition to having clarity to see the defect, I also have time to choose whether to engage with the defect or not. And, when I do act out a character defect, I am more likely to catch myself; I see the behavior with new eyes. I have even found a deep sense of humor arising within myself concerning some of the things I still catch myself doing. And with that kind of attention, the ego behind these compulsions becomes less strident, less domineering.

Step Seven is, indeed, the "turning point." This is where we begin to gain humility right in the presence of our character defects. Step Seven is the cauldron of alchemy where the heat and pressure of the conscious awareness of our defects creates a transformation of the defects into humility. And with this new-found humility, there comes a profound change in our attitude as we begin "to move out from ourselves and toward others and toward God."[40] As we often say in our meetings, the same person who walks into the meeting will drink again; the alcoholic must change to remain sober. Step Seven is where that change occurs most profoundly.

> *Do not let me hear*
> *Of the wisdom of old men, but rather of their folly,*
> *Their fear of fear and frenzy, their fear of*
> *possession,*
> *Of belonging to another, or to others, or to God.*
> *The only wisdom we can hope to acquire*
> *Is the wisdom of humility: humility is endless.*
>
> *T.S. Eliot*
> *Four Quartets*

---

[40] *Twelve and Twelve*, at p. 76.

Chapter 10
Those Defective Relationships

"Made a list of all persons we had harmed, and became willing to make amends to them all."

Step Eight

"Made direct amends to such people wherever possible, except when to do so would injure them or others."

Step Nine

Steps Eight and Nine again take us back in our personal history in order to identify our troubled personal relationships and make things right where we can. In Step Eight, we make another list, this time of "all persons we had harmed." The work of the Step is to become "willing to make amends to them all." In Step Nine, we will make contact with many of these people on the list for the purpose of making "direct amends to such people wherever possible, except when to do so would injure them or others."

We have already spent some time reviewing our past relationships with other people in the course of our inventories and admissions in the Fourth and Fifth Steps. Why are we coming back to these things, especially in light of how painful that previous work has already been for us? Because we have not yet actually done anything about those defective relationships. Our work in the program so far has not actually included the other people

The Spirituality of Sobriety

in our lives. We often hear in A.A. meetings that the Steps are in an order for a reason. I know I was not ready to effectively engage in amends to other people until after I had done some Sixth and Seventh Step work. It was in the light of the Seventh Step that I could see my character defects in the context of real relationships with people including family and close friends. With the measure of humility I gained in the Seventh Step, I was better able to realize the true extent of the hurt I had caused others. I was no longer so self-absorbed with my own pain and the remorse over my wrongs done to others. With humility as our guide, we are now able to "move out from ourselves toward others,"[1] and again review our past relationships from the perspective of those we hurt. "For the readiness to take the full consequences of our past acts, and to take responsibility for the well-being of others at the same time, is the very spirit of Step Nine."[2]

In reviewing the "causes and conditions" of our drinking in Chapter Four above, we noted that, while character defects were the "primary cause" of our drinking, defective relationships were the "immediate cause." After our inventories and admissions, we focused direct attention on the character defects in Steps Six and Seven. Now we turn our attention to the other cause of our alcoholism. In order to move past the mere symbol ("Bottles were only a symbol") and symptom ("Our liquor was but a symptom") of our true problem,[3] and to continue with the work on the underlying causes and conditions of our drinking, we will have to focus much attention on our defective relationships. After all, since "defective relationships with other human beings have nearly always been the immediate cause of our woes, including our alcoholism, no field of investigation could yield more satisfying and valuable rewards than this one."[4]

I also found the actual making of the amends crucial for my initial sobriety and continued recovery. This is the means by which we "sweep away the debris which has accumulated out of our effort to live on self-will

---

[1] *Twelve and Twelve*, at p. 76.
[2] *Twelve and Twelve*, at p. 87.
[3] *Big Book*, at pp. 103 and 64.
[4] *Twelve and Twelve*, at p. 80.

and run the show ourselves."[5] I was simply not going to be able to remain sober with the knowledge of my part in the "human wreckage" left in my wake, and not do something to try to alleviate some of this damage.[6] My pain over these things was "made more acute" because I could not use alcohol to kill it, as I had done in the past.[7] The effects of all this damage were continuing in my family relationships. Without some form of amends and making things right, the relationships with family members would have no basis for improvement. Things would only get worse. Continuing defective relationships with those close to me would certainly threaten any sobriety I may have gained. "Now we go out to our fellows and repair the damage done in the past."[8]

We begin this work by the making of the list. But we do not have to start from scratch. "We have a list of all persons we have harmed and to whom we are willing to make amends. We made it when we took inventory."[9] But, the only list the *Big Book* mentions in the Fourth Step discussion of inventories is the "grudge list," the list of our resentments toward people who we think hurt us.[10] The very same people on my resentment list from the Fourth Step now become the basis for my Eighth Step list for amends. The people I resent are often the same people I hurt. In concluding the discussion on the Fourth Step inventory, the *Big Book* mentions the dual nature of this list: "We have listed and analyzed our resentments…. We have listed the people we have hurt by our conduct, and are willing to straighten out the past if we can."[11] In dealing with my resentments, I found that I was not able to see the hurt I had caused others until I first was able to stop blaming them for my problems and forgive them for what I thought they had done to me. I should not be surprised now to find the same people showing up on both lists. It is this cycle of pain, this "she hurt me, I hurt her" nature of my relationships, that I now

---

[5] *Big Book*, at p. 76.
[6] *Twelve and Twelve*, at p. 77.
[7] *Twelve and Twelve*, at p. 39.
[8] *Big Book*, at p. 76.

[9] *Big Book*, at p. 76.
[10] *Big Book,* at pp. 64-67.
[11] *Big Book,* at p. 70.

see as the basis for the defective nature of all my relationships, leading to my alcoholism.

For the Eighth Step, we now refocus on the previous resentment list, perhaps adding additional names to it. And, equally important, we need to focus not so much on our own words and actions (the focus of the Fourth Step inventory), but on the impact these words and actions had on others (the Eighth Step list). In making this list, the alcoholic "ought to redouble his efforts to see how many people he has hurt, and in what ways."[12] So, to some extent, we are covering ground we already explored in the Fourth Step inventory. But now we are looking at what we find a bit differently, and we are double checking to make sure we did not miss anything the first time. From our previous inventory, we might go back over "all personal relationships which bring continuous or recurring trouble."[13] We might especially consider "our twisted relations with family, friends, and society at large."[14]

We are cautioned by the *Twelve and Twelve* that we are quite likely to encounter a number of obstacles in our attempt at making this list of all persons we have harmed. First is the issue of blame and forgiveness. "To escape looking at the wrongs we have done another, we resentfully focus on the wrong he has done us."[15] We become defensive and seek to hide our part by blaming the other for his part in the harm done. As we found back in Step Four in making our initial inventory: "Where other people were concerned, we had to drop the word 'blame' from our speech and thought."[16] The suggestion at the Eighth Step now goes a bit further for those situations where the other person's actions did contribute to the harm done: "If we are now about to ask forgiveness for ourselves, why shouldn't we start out by forgiving them, one and all?"[17]

Another obstacle is the fear and embarrassment we project at this point forward to our actually confronting the person we harmed and

---

[12] *Twelve and Twelve*, at p. 77.
[13] *Twelve and Twelve*, at p. 52.
[14] *Twelve and Twelve*, at p. 53.

[15] *Twelve and Twelve*, at p. 78.
[16] *Twelve and Twelve*, at p. 47.
[17] *Twelve and Twelve*, at p. 78.

admitting directly to the person "our wretched conduct."[18] At this point we should remember that we are just making the list now, not actually confronting the people. Here, we simply need to add the name to our list.

One more obstacle sometimes arises when we hide the harm we have done to others under deep denial, objecting that we were not all that bad to family, friends and employers. For the alcoholic, it simply is not possible to have completed a drinking career and be driven into recovery "under the lash of alcoholism," and not have left human wreckage in his wake. If nothing else, the alcoholic has harmed others by what he has not done – by failing to be available to others and take on the full array of responsibilities appropriate for his relationships. To get at this obstacle, the *Twelve and Twelve* suggests "a deep and honest search of our motives and actions."[19]

In looking at the actual harms we have done to the people on our list, we may frequently find that the situation is not all one-sided. It may not always be that we simply inflicted our character defect upon an unknowing and unsuspecting innocent bystander. Many of the people on our list will be people in ongoing relationship with us. As we already saw above, it may be that their conduct has contributed to the harm done. While this does not change the work we have to do in our making amends for our part, I do find it helpful for better identifying the harms done. In this regard, I find the *Twelve and Twelve's* definition of the word harm to be enlightening: "To define the word 'harm' in a practical way, we might call it the result of instincts in collision, which cause physical, mental, emotional, or spiritual damage to people."[20] Thus the harm done others may not arise from my own character defect; it may arise out of a primary instinctual need instead. And, the harm occurs because two instincts collide. So, the other person's instinctual need is involved, too. The definition contains no mention of blame or even responsibility. There is no measuring of who is more or less responsible for the "collision." It is simply a recognition of harm occurring to a person as a result of the instincts of two people colliding at a point in

[18] *Twelve and Twelve*, at p. 78.
[19] *Twelve and Twelve*, at p. 79.
[20] *Twelve and Twelve*, at p. 80.

time. The work for us here is to take responsibility for our part in the collision, and make things right as best we can. We do not try to justify or minimize our part by pointing out the other's involvement in the collision. That would be the other person's work, if he chose to take it on. However, it is our own recovery we are now working, not the other person's. "We shall want to hold ourselves to the course of admitting the things *we* have done, meanwhile forgiving the wrongs done us, real or fancied."[21]

There may be situations where this collision of instincts has caused us great emotional harm as well, even if the harm done the other person was not great. "Very deep, sometimes quite forgotten, damaging emotional conflicts persist below the level of consciousness. At the time of these occurrences, they may actually have given our emotions violent twists which have since discolored our personalities and altered our lives for the worse."[22] While our present work is directed toward the harm done other people, it is quite likely that our own hurt, buried away and ignored for years, will surface as we remember and reflect upon the same situations that caused the harm to the other person.

When our Eighth Step list is complete, we should pause before making actual contact with the people harmed for the making of amends. There is a good bit of preliminary work to be done first. We need to spend some time simply reflecting on the things on the list and getting to a "right attitude in which to proceed."[23] Then we need to make sure we ourselves have healed and grown enough to do this work without relapsing. Three times in the discussion of the Ninth Step we are cautioned to make amends to certain groups of people only as we gain sufficient degrees of sobriety:

Those who ought to be dealt with immediately – "as soon as we become reasonably confident that we can maintain our sobriety."[24]

---

[21] *Twelve and Twelve*, at pp. 81-82.
[22] *Twelve and Twelve*, at pp. 79-80.
[23] *Twelve and Twelve*, at p. 83.
[24] *Twelve and Twelve*, at p. 83.

Those Defective Relationships

Employers and Workmates – "First we will wish to be reasonably certain that we are on the A.A. beam."[25]

Those who have been seriously affected – "[a]s soon as we begin to feel confident in our new way of life and have begun, by our behavior and example, to convince those about us that we are indeed changing for the better."[26]

This is gut-wrenching spiritual work we are about to undertake. As we remember the difficulties and resistance we encountered in making the list, we will want to assure ourselves that our defensiveness, rationalizations, and blame do not resurface in the course of actually making the amend to the person we have harmed. We also need to consider the appropriate form the amend should take to make the best repair of the relationship that we can. "A remorseful mumbling that we are sorry won't fill the bill at all."[27] Finally, we need to carefully consider whether a direct amend itself may injure the person or others. If so, we need to rethink how to make the amend, if at all.

This taking of the Ninth Step is a matter we should conduct with great sensitivity. Up until now, our recovery work has involved only ourselves, our sponsors, perhaps an additional Fifth Step person to hear our admission, and God. At the Ninth Step, we begin to involve other people in our recovery work. And, these are not just any people. They are the very people we harmed in the course of our destructive drinking careers. Many of them will be family, friends, neighbors, employers and workmates with whom we are still in relationship, albeit defective. How we bring each of these individuals into our own recovery work in the course of the Ninth Step is a delicate matter. "Good judgment, a careful sense of timing, courage, and prudence – these are the qualities we shall need when we take Step Nine."[28] These were not qualities that I possessed in any great measure at the time I took the Ninth Step. I believe help from a sponsor is absolutely

---

[26] *Twelve and Twelve*, at p. 84.
Twelve and Twelve, at p. 85.

[27] *Big Book*, at p. 83.
[28] *Twelve and Twelve*, at p. 83.

critical for this Step. I was still involved in psychotherapy at the time I began my Ninth Step, so I included my therapist in planning amends for some of my most troubled family relationships. Discussions with others in recovery who have had similar situations may provide most helpful guidance. If there was ever a time in recovery to not do something alone, this is it! The last thing we want to do is cause further harm in the course of making an inappropriate amend to someone we had already hurt in the past. And we certainly do not want this work to overwhelm our new found sobriety and take us into a relapse. Good counsel from others who have been this way before is the safe direction through these shoals.

Although we have completed the making of our amends, we are not done with our recovery work on personal relations. The making of the list and the amends completes the first two parts of Steps Eight and Nine. We are now ready to take on the third part of these Steps: "having thus cleaned away the debris of the past, we consider how, with our newfound knowledge of ourselves, we may develop the best possible relations with every human being we know."[29] Not to minimize the making of the amends, but this work at the third part of these Steps is what I think the *Twelve and Twelve* is referring back to when it says: "This is a very large order. It is a task which we may perform with increasing skill, but never really finish."[30] And, I believe it is because of this work to come of making "best possible relations with every human being we know," that the Eighth Step has come to mean in A.A. experience "the beginning of the end of isolation from our fellows and from God."[31]

Personal relationships become a window through which we can gain greater visibility into our character defects as well our basic nature. This newfound knowledge may be quite profound. While we have certainly gained much knowledge of ourselves from the Fourth Step inventory and our other recovery work, the knowledge we may gain here is different:

---

[29] *Twelve and Twelve*, at p. 77.
[30] *Twelve and Twelve*, at p. 77.
[31] *Twelve and Twelve*, at p. 82.

Those Defective Relationships

Calm, thoughtful reflection upon personal relations can deepen our insight. We can go far beyond those things which were superficially wrong with us, to see those flaws which were basic, flaws which sometimes were responsible for the whole pattern of our lives. Thoroughness, we have found, will pay – and pay handsomely.[32]

One flaw we should certainly find is the egomania that causes alcoholics to seek either to dominate other people or to be overdependent upon them. This is a cycle that has prevented us from forming true partnerships with the people in our lives. "We have not once sought to be one in a family, to be a friend among friends, to be a worker among workers, to be a useful member of society.... Of true brotherhood we had small comprehension."[33] We should also be able to identify incessant and unreasonable demands that we make upon others. We might also become more aware of sensitive areas where we too easily develop hurt feelings.[34]

Finally, we work to apply this deep knowledge about ourselves to our new relationships in sobriety, with the goal of making each relationship the best possible. This is another one of those lifetime jobs "which we may perform with increasing skill, but never really finish."[35] The *Twelve and Twelve* acknowledges that "[t]his is a very large order."[36] Here is where we see that our recovery work broadens far beyond just getting sober and not drinking. We are far away from working to stop a compulsion to drink. Our recovery work now has us "[l]earning how to live in the greatest peace, partnership, and brotherhood with all men and women, of whatever description."[37] This work starts at the Eighth and Ninth Steps, based on our newfound knowledge about ourselves. But the work will continue in the last part of the Twelfth Step as part of the practice of the principles in all our affairs. Much of that work will be concerned with the building of better relationships based on the appropriate satisfaction of our instinctual needs.

---

[32] *Twelve and Twelve*, at p. 80.
[33] *Twelve and Twelve*, at p. 53.
[34] *Twelve and Twelve*, at pp. 53, 115-17.

[35] *Twelve and Twelve*, at p. 77.
[36] *Twelve and Twelve*, at p. 77.
[37] *Twelve and Twelve*, at p. 77.

The Spirituality of Sobriety

By moving into the realm of "best relationships," have we left recovery behind and moved into psychology and counseling? Or is this now ethics and religion, like a Sunday School class at church? Have we exceeded the bounds of a proper focus on legitimate issues bearing on the recovery from alcoholism? Not if we keep in mind that the immediate cause of our alcoholism was those defective relationships. Having made our amends for the harms we caused in those defective relationships and repaired the damage as best we could, we now must learn how to put together functional, working, and satisfying relationships to avoid a return to further defective relationships and, thus, a relapse to alcoholism. Yes, this work is very much about my on-going recovery from alcoholism. In fact, I may choose to think of this as my relapse prevention therapy!

The end of the Ninth Step brings us to the Promises, a section of the *Big Book* often read aloud at A.A. meetings. If we have been diligently working our way through the Steps, and are making amends, then "we will be amazed before we are half way through."[38] And then we are given The Promises – one of the most precious sections of the *Big Book* to alcoholics in recovery everywhere:

We are going to know a new freedom and a new happiness. We will not regret the past nor wish to shut the door on it. We will comprehend the word serenity and we will know peace. No matter how far down the scale we have gone, we will see how our experience can benefit others. That feeling of uselessness and self-pity will disappear. We will lose interest in selfish things and gain interest in our fellows. Self-seeking will slip away. Our whole attitude and outlook upon life will change. Fear of people and of economic insecurity will leave us. We will intuitively know how to handle situations which used to baffle us. We will suddenly realize that God is doing for us what we could not do for ourselves.

---

[38] *Big Book*, at p. 83.

Are these extravagant promises? We think not. They are being fulfilled among us – sometimes quickly, sometimes slowly. They will always materialize if we work for them.[39]

The kind of life laid out in the Promises is the reverse of our lives during our drinking career. It is the kind of life laying before us, as we continue with the rest of the Steps.

---

[39] *Big Book*, at pp. 83-84.

Chapter 11
Achieving Some Emotional Balance (Your Friends Will Thank You!)

"Continued to take personal inventory and when we were wrong promptly admitted it."

Step Ten

Having made amends as best he can to those he has harmed, the recovering alcoholic is now on the verge of launching into the rest of his life. At the Tenth Step, the focus changes from the past to the present. From here, we are not so directly concerned with the things from the past. We will continue to gain additional insight into our past as we grow more spiritually. Things we just could not see before will open to us as we are ready to receive them. But, in the Tenth Step the emphasis of our recovery program shifts from the past to the present. While the lessons we learned in our past will form the part of our story about "what we used to be like…," we now begin to focus on the part of our story about "what we are like now."[1]

---

[1] *Big Book*, at p. 58.

The Spirituality of Sobriety

The Tenth Step says, "Continued to take personal inventory and when we were wrong promptly admitted it." The Tenth Step is the acid test for our new way of life: "can we stay sober, keep in *emotional balance*, and live to good purpose under all conditions?"[2] I picture the transition from the hard recovery work of the first Nine Steps to the emotional balance sought in the Tenth Step as a boy on a bicycle. My entrance into recovery finds me and the bike wrecked in the ditch and not looking very well. The early Steps are all about getting the bike out of the ditch and getting the boy and the bike put back together again. At the Tenth Step, I am on the bike again, peddling and moving forward. The Tenth Step is about keeping my balance on the bike so I do not end up wrecked in the ditch again. It's about small moment-by-moment and day-by-day adjustments to keep the bike stable and moving forward in the right direction. I often picture these subtle adjustments in aviation terms. The jet leaving New York City bound for San Francisco does not simply set a course and fly directly there. In fact, the jet is never on course for San Francisco. Rather, it is always a little bit off course. The pilots constantly make minor course corrections to keep the jet moving in the overall correct direction. It's like driving your car on a highway where you find yourself constantly making subtle adjustments at the steering wheel notwithstanding that you are on a long straight section of highway. Having gotten sober and made some progress in the recovery program, we do not simply set our course and put our lives on autopilot. We need constant course corrections during each day, and the Tenth Step is the instrument we use to show us the way.

The *Twelve and Twelve* suggests three different formats for ongoing inventories. The first is the spot-check inventory, "taken at any time of the day, whenever we find ourselves getting tangled up."[3] The second is the daily review at the end of the day. The *Twelve and Twelve* focuses its discussion of the Tenth Step primarily on these two inventories. The third one is a more occasional or annual check-up, on our own or with a

---

[2] *Twelve and Twelve*, at p. 88 (emphasis added).
[3] *Twelve and Twelve*, at p. 89.

Achieving Some Emotional Balance

sponsor or spiritual advisor. The focus here is on progress since the last inventory. Many A.A.'s, including myself, also use this format for a self-searching in regard to a particular issue, such as a recurring relationship issue, or a job-related problem, or a difficult attitude. Recovery retreats offered by many religious organizations are a wonderful opportunity to take on this work in a spiritual and supportive atmosphere.

Why all this insistence on inventories? Can't we just get on with our life after all the work we've already done to see and acknowledge our past mistakes and make them right as best we can? The Tenth Step is just putting into a rather formal practice a habit of self-reflection that we must have in order to maintain our emotional balance and a meaningful sobriety. Without this process of "self-searching," "self-appraisal," and "self-examination," we lack the knowledge we need to make adjustments in our daily living to maintain our balance on the bicycle.[4] It is the spot-check inventory in particular, supported by the daily inventory, that gives us this real-time data that we can use to make our course corrections during our day-to-day living. It only feels awkward at first because we are so unused to doing anything at all like this. In the past, we did not focus our attention on our role in our difficulties; rather, we just blamed other people for the problems and talked to other drunks at the bar about how our lives were someone else's fault! Now we are putting into daily, ongoing practice the new approach to our problems used so successfully in our previous work on Steps Four through Nine. There is a strong Buddhist flavor to this Tenth Step practice – it seems to me to have similarities to the practice of looking deeply and the mindfulness teachings of Vietnamese Buddhist monk Thich Nhat Hanh.[5]

The daily review inventory format seems to come easier for a lot of alcoholics. There is a natural time of reflection over the past day that occurs in the evening for many people. Here, we just need to assure that the focus of the reflection is on our own actions, not those of others. This is

---

[4] *Twelve and Twelve*, at pp. 88-89.
[5] Thich Nhat Hanh, *The Miracle of Mindfulness* (Boston: Beacon Press, 1976).

self-examination, not blame of others. The particular focus in the daily review is on our motives underlying the actions and words of the day. We have the time at the end of the day to be a bit reflective in examining these underlying motives. In some cases, our motive will be readily apparent. We can then use a visualization exercise to see how our behavior may have been improved, and then ask help of our Higher Power to make this change tomorrow. Of course, amends may be necessary as well. In other cases, we may have some difficulty seeing our true motive if we have hidden or disguised it under justifications or rationalizations. Spending some time with particular events of the day that keep coming to mind, without listening to the mental explanation or commentary that may run with it, can help clarify our true motive in the event. In my experience, the truth of the event tends to be simple and something basic, whereas the rationalization or justification tends to be long-winded, with many points to be made. Waiting for the simple truth can help achieve clarity of our true motives. With this knowledge, we can again make our necessary course corrections and amends, if necessary.[6]

The spot-check inventory is the one that tends to be more difficult to get into regular practice. There is no particular time of day for this one. Rather, we take this inventory right in the midst of an emotional disturbance. "The quick inventory is aimed at our daily ups and downs, especially those where people or new events throw us off balance and tempt us to make mistakes."[7] Its purpose is to help us quiet the storm. Hopefully, the result will be the exercise of self-restraint and the avoidance of an "emotional hangover" from "excesses of negative emotion."[8] We are trying to catch ourselves right in the midst of our own disturbance, but before we have said or done things that will throw us off balance and threaten our sobriety. We are trying to first avoid the "emotional booby traps" so we can make better, more meaningful choices about our behavior, instead of unconscious reactions.[9]

---

[6] *Twelve and Twelve*, at p. 94.
[7] *Twelve and Twelve*, at p. 92.
[8] *Twelve and Twelve*, at p. 88.
[9] *Twelve and Twelve*, at p. 91.

Achieving Some Emotional Balance

It is difficult to bring this change of focus away from the words and actions of others back to ourselves when the emotions are running high and we are intently engaged with the people or events that are the subject of the disturbance. The *Twelve and Twelve* provides a tool, in the form of a deep spiritual truth, that I have found extremely effective in bringing this change of focus: "It is a spiritual axiom that every time we are disturbed, no matter what the cause, there is something wrong *with us*."[10] Notice that this truth does not deny that the other person involved is "wrong" also. In fact, the next sentence explaining the spiritual axiom expressly assumes the other person has caused hurt and thus been in the wrong: "If somebody hurts us and we are sore, we are in the wrong also."[11]

There is nothing in the Tenth Step that denies, or even questions for a moment that others may act inappropriately and that we may have been hurt by their actions. The Tenth Step merely asks us to broaden our gaze to see our part in the wrong. We are not passive victims in life. The spiritual truth leading to emotional balance is that we have a role in every emotional disturbance we experience, notwithstanding any involvement of others. "But it is clear that we made our own misery. God didn't do it."[12] Continuing reflection on the spiritual axiom of our own involvement in our emotional disturbances has led me right back to the Third Step, seeing the spiritual axiom as an application of the basic self-centeredness that has been the root of my troubles from the beginning. At this point, it is well to remember the *Big Book's* admonition: "So our troubles, we think, are basically of our own making."[13] As we open ourselves to that self-knowledge we grow spiritually. We do not grow by examining the motives and actions of others; we only grow by self-examination.

If our spot-check inventory has been successful in the midst of an emotional disturbance, then the first thing we will find is the development of some self-restraint and self-control.[14] "We learned that if we were seriously disturbed, our *first* need was to quiet that disturbance, regardless

---

[10] *Twelve and Twelve*, at p. 90.
[11] *Twelve and Twelve*, at p. 90.
[12] *Big Book*, at p. 133.
[13] *Big Book*, at p. 62.
[14] *Twelve and Twelve*, at p. 91.

of who or what we thought caused it."[15] Now we are not reacting to what has been said or done to us, so we gain time to consider our response before saying or doing something we will later regret. This benefit, itself, is worth the price of the spot-check inventory, but there is more. In that time, we also gain perspective on the situation. We get a chance to see our role in the situation before we react. We also may see that our perception of things may itself be based on our own disturbed emotional nature. Things may not really be the way we are perceiving them at the moment. Motives we have attributed to others may have been projected from our own fear and negative feelings.

As Carl Jung once said, "Your vision will become clear only when you look into your heart.... Who looks outside, dreams. Who looks inside, awakens." However, if I still believe the disturbance is caused by the behavior of others, I can look to our teachings on acceptance and ask myself, "why do I lack the ability to accept conditions I cannot change?"[16] We can go even further. Within this broader, but self-restrained context, we may also gain an enlarged view on the others involved in the disturbance. "Finally, we begin to see that all people, including ourselves, are to some extent emotionally ill as well as frequently wrong, and then we approach true tolerance and see what real love for our fellows actually means."[17] We now get to make a choice about our response, taking into consideration our new understanding. We also get to consider the impact of our contemplated response on our own emotional balance and sobriety before we say or do anything that would steer the bike toward the ditch again.

If we are able to use each disturbance as an opportunity to broaden our view on those around us, we have the opportunity to grow into a whole new attitude toward people: "It will become more and more evident as we go forward that it is pointless to become angry, or to get hurt by people who, like us, are suffering from the pains of growing up."[18] As a result of this realization, I find myself in fewer emotional disturbances requiring a

---

[15] *Twelve and Twelve*, at p. 47.
[16] *Twelve and Twelve*, at p. 52.
[17] *Twelve and Twelve*, at p. 92.

[18] *Twelve and Twelve*, at p. 92.

Tenth Step inventory. And when the disturbances do still arise, they are of less intensity. However, we are cautioned, "Such a radical change in our outlook will take time, maybe a lot of time."[19] It is one thing to say it. It is something else completely to find my reaction to the offensive words or conduct of others actually changing in line with this "radical change" in my own attitude such that I respond from love and tolerance instead of reacting in hurt and anger. The *Twelve and Twelve* gives us some guidance on what our reactions will begin to look like if we are gaining this new outlook:

Unreasonable Demands: "We can try to stop making unreasonable demands upon those we love."

Kindness: "We can show kindness where we had shown none."

Understanding and Helpfulness: "With those we dislike we can begin to practice justice and courtesy, perhaps going out of our way to understand and help them."[20]

I believe this "radical change" in attitude toward greater compassion and tolerance of others involved in my emotional disturbances is the deeper truth of Step Ten. However, to the extent I find myself stuck with some concern about "fault" in the disturbance, to the extent that who "caused" the disturbance still seems important (especially if my own role in the disturbance has been particularly glaring), then I find the challenge of a duality of response provided by the *Twelve and Twelve* to greatly simplify my thinking about the disturbance. Once I have gained the self-restraint and some clarity about the situation, then there are only two responses: "a willingness to admit when the fault is ours, and an equal willingness to forgive when the fault is elsewhere."[21] Of course, most disturbances are likely to be a mixture of fault. In any event, there are only

---

[19] *Twelve and Twelve*, at p. 92.
[20] *Twelve and Twelve*, at p. 93 (emphasis added).
[21] *Twelve and Twelve*, at p. 91.

The Spirituality of Sobriety

two meaningful responses for me in the context of my Tenth Step practice: I either admit, or I forgive. I do not justify and I do not blame. In the midst of the disturbance, I have not even found it helpful to explain or seek clarification. But I have found admissions and forgiveness to be effective in calming the disturbance all around. And if these are the only two choices, it makes finding "the next right thing to do" much easier when I find myself in the midst of emotional disturbance.

I now see this change in my reactions to disturbances as a progression from the spiritual axiom of my own involvement in the disturbance, to a gaining of a new perspective on each situation, to the "radical change" in my own attitude toward others involved in the disturbances. To get this change into my gut, where I actually respond differently, has taken a great deal of time. And sometimes I still "fall into the error of our old ways," but the disturbances are still less frequent and of less intensity, and I find my way out much more quickly today.[22] To achieve some confidence in my ability to avoid relapse, and to truly enjoy a continuing quality sobriety, I have found this need for emotional balance in disturbances to be absolutely critical. "We can't stand it if we hate deeply. The idea that we can be possessively loving of a few, can ignore the many, and can continue to fear or hate *anybody*, has to be abandoned, if only a little at a time."[23]

But what about the "real" emotion we are feeling at the moment? Do we just stuff the anger we feel? Shouldn't we express the anger? Aren't there times when the anger is appropriate or justified? The *Twelve and Twelve* does not enter this debate. It simply recounts the consequences for the alcoholic of acting out anger, and concludes: "We have found that justified anger ought to be left to those better qualified to handle it."[24] The impact of carrying a resentment is the same for the alcoholic "whether our resentments were justified or not."[25] The alcoholic's decision to act out anger must be made in the context of the impact of anger and resentments on her ability to remain sober. "Anger, that occasional luxury of more

---

[22] *Twelve and Twelve*, at p. 91.
[23] *Twelve and Twelve*, at p. 93.
[24] *Twelve and Twelve*, at p. 90.
[25] *Twelve and Twelve*, at p. 90.

Achieving Some Emotional Balance

balanced people, could keep us on an emotional jag indefinitely. These emotional 'dry benders' often led straight to the bottle."[26] It is in the context of our desire for continued sobriety and to avoid potential relapse that the alcoholic enters the debate on the appropriate use of anger. For us, it is clearly dangerous ground.

We may find that our anger is nothing more than "the smoke screen under which we were hiding some of our defects while we blamed others for them."[27] The anger could be the result of our own projection, rather than a true response to a correctly perceived situation. I have found that anger for me is always covering another, deeper emotion that I am reluctant to acknowledge. I now refer to my anger as a "cheap emotion," always presenting itself first, but not having much substance. As I stay with the anger, neither acting it out or stuffing it, but just allowing it to be present to me, I invariably find other, deeper emotions arising that are more real and reflect my true situation.

The first time I experienced this rising depth of emotion was quite dramatic for me. I was on business travel, driving to a large unfamiliar airport that was under construction. The temporary signs seemed to indicate the way to the airline I was flying that evening. I had left myself little time to make the flight, and hurried from the parking lot to the terminal. Once inside, I could not locate the airline. Upon making enquiry, I was informed that my airline was at a different terminal on the opposite end of this large airport, and I would need to await a shuttle bus outside to get there. Unfortunately, I only had ten minutes to departure time and knew I would never make it. My flight was the last one to my destination that evening. I had a very important early morning meeting the next day. The anger welled up. My normal behavior pattern would have been to throw my bags down on the floor and yell at the person at the counter about how the misleading signs outside were all wrong and couldn't they do something about getting proper signs in place! Instead of acting this out, I just stood

---

[26] *Twelve and Twelve*, at p. 90.
[27] *Twelve and Twelve*, at p. 59.

where I was, took a couple of deep breaths, and then realized how sad I felt that I would not be able to make the meeting.

As the sadness arose from a deeper level, I more gently set my bags down and thanked the person for the information, briefly explaining that I would never make it to the other terminal in time for the last flight of the day to my destination. My body and words were now speaking sadness, not anger. This sadness dissipated the easily ignited, but now extinguishing, anger. And then the miracle occurred that made this disturbance so memorable to me. A chauffeur awaiting someone at that terminal walked up to me and said he had overheard the situation. The flight he was awaiting had been delayed, so he would be happy to run me around to the other terminal in his limo parked right outside the door! We ran to his vehicle and he sped around the airport, dropping me right in front of the correct terminal just in time to make the flight. The lesson I took from this situation was that the deeper emotions allow others to come to my assistance, setting up the possibility for a miracle to occur. When I choose the easier anger in the situation, I drive people away from me and preclude the arrival of assistance, making miracles much more difficult in my life. After all, if I had thrown my bags down on the floor and gone into my usual temper tantrum, it is not at all likely that the chauffeur would have been drawn to me and volunteered his assistance. I saw this connection between getting to the deeper emotions under the anger and the greater possibility of miracle and unexpected solutions showing up in my life. This life lesson is of critical importance to the quality of my life and sobriety. It is the deeper work of the Tenth Step.

Sometime later, I attended a weekend recovery retreat, and I took the opportunity to do a more extended Tenth Step inventory on the depth of my emotions underlying the surface anger. I recalled several past situations in which anger had overwhelmed me. I found the anger still present just from my memory of the details of the situations. In each case, I spent time with the anger almost like a meditation or, as the Buddhists might say, looking deeply at the feeling and its roots. I did not try to "do" anything with, or about, the anger. I just let it be what it was for a period of time. I did work at quieting the running commentary and explanation that my mind would add as further fuel to the fire of the anger and indignation. I tried to just stay with my immediate memory of the situation and the feeling of anger arising from it, not the thoughts about it. I recalled a spiritual exercise in which we think of emotions as messengers from deeper areas within ourselves that show up to give us important information.

> This being human is a guest house.
> Every morning a new arrival.
>
> A joy, a depression, a meanness,
> some momentary awareness comes
> as an unexpected visitor.
>
> Welcome and entertain them all!
> Even if they're a crowd of sorrows,
> who violently sweep your house
> empty of its furniture, still,
> treat each guest honorably.
> He may be clearing you out
> for some new delight.
>
> The dark thought, the shame, the malice,
> meet them at the door laughing
> and invite them in.
>
> Be grateful for whoever comes,
> because each has been sent
> as a guide from beyond.[28]

---

[28] *Rumi, The Book of Love*, at pp. 179-80.

The Spirituality of Sobriety

The gist of the exercise is to allow the emotion to present itself, deliver its message, and then move on through us. They are visitors, house guests, not permanent inhabitants of the house, and certainly not the host or hostess of the house. There is a time for their arrival, and there is a time for their departure. In the meantime, they are guests in our house to be treated honorably.

As I stayed with the anger, neither stuffing nor acting out, just giving it space to be, and deliver its message, I began to gain some insight into the anger itself as well as deeper emotions as they began to surface. I could see the anger as an initial response, like a trigger reaction, readying me physically and mentally to defend against an attack by triggering the fight or flight response. Having sprung the trigger, the anger has done its job. The problem for me was getting stuck at the anger level and acting out on it. I was believing that the anger arose from, and was justified by, the actions or words or the perceived intentions of other people. Now I could see that the anger was simply my own trigger response to a situation as I perceived it; the anger was not imposed upon me by others. The anger fully served its purpose after triggering the fight or flight reaction readying me for an attack. My work was now to remain conscious of the anger as my own reaction, avoid the denial, and keep moving in the space I had provided around the emotion itself.

As I continued seeking space around the anger, I gradually found another emotion inevitably beginning to surface – sadness. Just like my airport experience, sadness always came up under the anger. I now saw the anger as a pushing of people away from me, and the sadness as drawing people toward me, creating the opportunity to obtain help from others and connect with them at a real-life level. The sadness seemed to open another way outside of myself, like service work does. My heart seemed to open to a neglected or ignored sense of longing for real connection to people. So, again, I stayed with this feeling of sadness around each situation, giving it space in its turn to deliver its message to me, and then move on. I did not resist it or try to explain it. Then, into this space, came the fear. This is what

114

each situation was really about for me. There was always an underlying fear about something that was triggered by the situation. It was really about something in me.

The anger brought the energy and attention to the area, pushing other things away as less important so this area in my life could be seen and dealt with. Then the sadness brought the connection with, and assistance from, other people. The underlying fear was always about losing something or not getting something I wanted. Sometimes it seemed to be about a deep longing for something that was missing in my life. The feeling of loss always seemed to be connected to a sense of separateness. The sadness helped open me to people around me, helping to alleviate this sense of separateness, and calming the fear. In some situations I was able to even go below the fear. These situations involved the loss of significant things in my life. The feeling below the fear and separateness was a deep sense of regret over the loss, like a mourning or grieving over loss. If the loss was a result of my own poor behavior, I often found remorse arising in relationship to my part in the loss.

While I was attending to this work on the retreat, I encountered deep resistance to uncovering these deeper layers of emotion and grief. There was something in me that did not want go here. I wanted to push this troubling sense of my own inadequacy and separateness away from me, push it into my unconscious and avoid the pain of it all. The depth of these feelings was directly challenging my limited sense of self, the little self, or my ego. I began to see my brokenness and defectiveness in a new light. I had no protection or defense, and I could feel walls within me beginning to crumble. No outward enemy or judge could so effectively, efficiently and completely destroy my defenses and undermine all the protective structures I had built around my limited sense of self. I found the rising sense of regret and remorse moving right through the peripheral defenses to the heart of my self-centeredness and ego-centricity. Amazing – more Third Step work!

The Spirituality of Sobriety

But this still was not the end of this retreat experience for me. The inventory of emotions continued. Into the fear, regret and remorse came a gentle flooding of love and compassion. Not from anyone in particular, but just from all around me, as if I were surrounded by a loving presence in the room with me. Where I had previously felt my walls crumbling, this new loving presence had direct and immediate access to my deeper sense of self. I felt cared for and connected at a deep level. Everything was ok in all of the universe. And from this rising awareness of love and compassion, I could see no defense, no escape, no protection. But no enemy either. No fight, no fighter. Only love. The regret and remorse opened me to both the receiving and giving of compassion. I could now feel the compassion at a much greater depth. I saw compassion as love in action. When this love acts, responds or simply is, I experience it as compassion. And in this compassion I find complete acceptance of myself and others, and a sense of wonderment at the greatness of life within us. A fullness and completeness. And here I come to rest. All struggling is ceased. No defending. No fear. All is left behind, willingly. Laughingly! And then a deep, profound joy, a joy with tears, flooded me.

This process of moving through emotions has been discussed by psychologists. John Welwood, a clinical psychologist and psychotherapist and author of several works on psychology and spiritual growth, has written:

> In opening to our anger, we also find other feelings underneath it
> – sorrow, fear, or hurt – that are calling for attention and
> concern. And if we look still further, we often find, hidden deep
> within our rage, some long forgotten longing of the soul that we
> have given up on, because it was consistently frustrated in the
> past. Freeing up this desire can help us find direction, especially
> in times when we feel lost.[29]

---

[29] John Welwood, *Love and Awakening* (New York: Harper Collins, 1996), at p. 196.

Achieving Some Emotional Balance

So, the question is not whether to stuff our anger or act it out. Rather, the question is: What is the real emotion? In my experience, as I just allow the anger to be, I consistently find a more real emotion coming to the surface. Then the anger simply dissipates and I am left with a different emotion altogether. Now I can authentically express this deeper emotion, without either stuffing or acting out the anger.

When I avoid the conscious awareness of the negative emotion under the anger, I find myself projecting the problem onto someone else. When I make no attempt to avoid the deeper emotion, I now see clearly my role in the emotional disturbance that started me on this process of looking deeply at the anger. My alcohol addiction had helped to anesthetize the pain associated with not attending to the negative emotions underlying the anger. For the alcoholic in this situation, his troubles are "now made more acute because he cannot use alcohol to kill the pain."[30] I have fairly consistently found the following projections for the ignored inner state:

Inner State	*Projection*
Anger	Frustrated with others
Sadness	Disappointed with or offended by others
Fear	Upset with others
Regret	Blame, judgment, criticism of others

Because of this fairly consistent link with the projection, I can now return to my inner state even if I am not immediately aware of the negative emotion that is presenting itself under the anger. All I have to do is note the projection I am making onto the other person. By simply acknowledging the deeper emotion based on my projection, and giving it space, I am usually able to connect with it, and then successfully move through it.

I have seen a lot of angry alcoholics come into the A.A. meetings over the years. Those who stay have always changed. One fellow in particular

---

[30] *Twelve and Twelve*, at p. 39.

The Spirituality of Sobriety

became quite a legend in my home group. He was a big, burly construction worker, barrel-chested with upper arms as big around as my thighs. He would sit at the table taking up four or five chairs, not because of how big he was, but because of his boiling rage that drove people to sit a distance from him. When he first started sharing at the meeting, there was so much anger in his voice I half expected to see him throw a chair across the room. Everything was about what other people had unjustly done to him, and why his whole life was someone else's fault. As he continued to come to meetings the miracle started occurring. In less than a year, he was our self-appointed, unofficial greeter. It was impossible to get in the door without a heartfelt handshake or a hug from this man. He became a huge teddy bear. At his one year anniversary, his wife and two little children, often in his lap or snuggled up to him, attended the meeting. I cried when he picked up his medallion. I don't think there was a dry eye in the room.

From this experience, I began asking, "Where does the anger go?" I now recognized that my own anger was breaking up. I could see the miracle happening to others, too. My own experience involved connecting to the deeper emotions and developing a more complete spectrum of emotions. I have heard others share that acceptance and letting things go have lessened the anger for them. Others share that things that used to cause a disturbance for them simply do not seem so important anymore. In the context of the miracle of my sobriety and ongoing recovery, the relative importance of things has certainly changed for me. Rumi spoke of this change in relative importance of things in the context of the Beloved when he wrote this love poem to God:

Come to the orchard in spring.
There is light and wine and sweethearts
in the pomegranate flowers.

If you do not come, these do not matter.
If you do come, these do not matter.[31]

---

[31] Coleman Barks, tr., *The Book of Love,* at p. 91.

118

Achieving Some Emotional Balance

I think of my sobriety as this poem. If I am not sober, then none of the other things matter because I will lose them anyway. If I am sober, then none of the other things matter in the sense that the miracle of my sobriety transcends all the other things. Either way, the relative importance of things to me is forever changed by the miracle of sobriety. "Being wrecked in the same vessel, being restored and united under one God, with hearts and minds attuned to the welfare of others, the things which matter so much to some people no longer signify much to them. How could they?"[32]

There is one other way in which I think of emotional balance today. So far, we have been talking about calming the extremes of negative emotions, finding deeper emotions, and transforming negative emotions to positive emotions of compassion and tolerance. I also think of emotional balance in terms of "congruence," a term developed by Carl Rogers to describe a person who is emotionally the same at all levels. No matter what the person is feeling, "we sense that he is the same at all levels – in what he is experiencing at an organismic level, in his awareness at the conscious level, and in his words and communications."[33] Emotional balance in this sense means I am consciously aware of the very feeling I am experiencing physically, and my communication to others accurately reflects that same feeling. A Gnostic saying of Jesus identifies this vertical alignment with the Kingdom of God: "When you make the two into one, and when you make the inner like the outer and the outer like the inner, and the upper like the lower…, then you will enter the kingdom."[34] This congruence may become a basis for an increased spirituality, but it certainly will bring new balance to our relationships with the people in our lives.

> We say of such a person that we know "exactly where he stands." We tend to feel comfortable and secure in such a relationship. With another person we recognize that what he is saying is almost certainly a front or a façade. We wonder what he *really* feels, what

---

[32] *Big Book*, at p. 161.
[33] *On Becoming A Person,* at p. 283.

[34] Marvin Meyer, *The Gospel of Thomas* (San Francisco: Harper, 1992), at p. 35.

119

The Spirituality of Sobriety

he is really experiencing, behind this façade. We may also wonder if *he* knows what he really feels, recognizing that he may be quite unaware of the feelings he is actually experiencing. With such a person we tend to be cautious and wary. It is not the kind of relationship in which defenses can be dropped or in which significant learning and change can occur.[35]

My own experience confirms to me over and over that my relationships invariably improve as I "make the inner like the outer," as I achieve this emotionally-balanced congruence. With better relationships around me, I find, in turn, that staying in emotional balance is easier as I am not experiencing those extremes of negative emotions.

The *Big Book* provides a more cursory discussion of the practice of the Tenth Step. In the course of that discussion, it places the inventory and admissions work of this Step in the context of our developing spirituality, and links this with our ongoing sobriety: "We are not cured of alcoholism. What we really have is a daily reprieve contingent on the maintenance of our spiritual condition."[36] It is the practice of the Tenth Step that helps me maintain the spiritual condition that provides the daily reprieve. The *Big Book* also provides a wonderful description of the freedom we experience as we achieve our daily reprieve as the result of an ongoing Tenth Step practice: And we have ceased fighting anything or anyone – even alcohol. For by this time sanity will have returned. We will seldom be interested in liquor. If tempted, we recoil from it as from a hot flame. We react sanely and normally, and we will find that this has happened automatically. We will see that our new attitude toward liquor has been given us without any thought or effort on our part. It just comes! That is the miracle of it. We are not fighting it, neither are we avoiding temptation. We feel as though we had been placed in a position of neutrality – safe and protected. We

---

[35] *On Becoming A Person,* at p. 283.
[36] *Big Book*, at p. 85.

have not even sworn off. Instead, the problem has been removed.
It does not exist for us. We are neither cocky nor are we afraid.
That is our experience. That is how we react so long as we keep
in fit spiritual condition.[37]

What a wonderful state of mind and body for the alcoholic to achieve. This is why the Twelve Step program works: The recovering alcoholic can achieve this newfound state which is not otherwise available to him by his own unaided efforts. How appropriate it is that we are asked to move right into the Eleventh Step where, by prayer and meditation, we seek to improve our conscious contact with the Higher Power that has brought us to this new state of freedom from the compulsion to drink. If the freedom from the compulsion is contingent upon our spiritual condition, then we do well to take action in order to improve our awareness of this vitally important relationship with our Higher Power.

---

[37] *Big Book*, at pp. 84-85.

Chapter 12
Prayer and Meditation in Recovery

"Sought through prayer and meditation…."

Step Eleven

"We shouldn't be shy on this matter of prayer," the *Big Book* cautions us.[1] But we are shy. In my experience, prayer and meditation are not frequent topics of A.A. discussion meetings. Our Step meetings on the Eleventh Step are often "vague about this matter."[2] I recently sat in an Eleventh Step meeting at my home group and listened as we went around the room with one person after another talking honestly about how little time or effort they put into prayer and meditation. They did not feel that they were really doing very much to work this Step. Some talked of being more connected with the Step in earlier recovery, but that prayer and meditation time had taken a back seat to the seemingly more pressing activities of the day. At several other A.A. meetings I've attended regularly, people shared about holding deep resentments. Although they knew that prayer for the person was the answer to gain release from the resentment, they did not know how to pray or were unwilling to pray. This happened so many times that I began to share a simple prayer that has worked for me in removing resentments:

---

[1] *Big Book*, at p. 85.
[2] *Big Book*, at p. 86.

The Spirituality of Sobriety

> May I be at peace
> May my heart remain open
> May I awaken to the light of my own true nature
> May I be healed
> May I be a source of healing to all Beings.

Then the prayer is repeated as follows, specifically focused on the person toward whom I hold the resentment:

> May you be at peace
> May your heart remain open
> May you awaken to the light of your own true nature
> May you be healed
> May you be a source of healing to all Beings.

Several people thanked me after these meetings and asked for the prayer again so they could write it down.

These things started me wondering where we were in Eleventh Step practice. In my own recovery, I found prayer and meditation an absolute necessity. This was where I found my first serenity. My sponsor used to tell me repeatedly: "Gregg, you just don't see the situation clearly." It was prayer and meditation, along with his guidance, that helped bring clarity to me. This was where I tapped the power to move myself repeatedly through the Steps, applying them over and over to all my faults and problems, including my "problems other than alcohol."[3] Prayer and meditation did become like "air, food, or sunshine" for me, and I knew this Eleventh Step practice was providing "vitally needed support" to my mind, emotions, and intuition.[4] Of this, I was, and remain, quite convinced. Today, in long-term sobriety, I find my Eleventh Step practice to be the leading edge of my continued recovery and spiritual growth.

This all became quite clear to me at an A.A. meeting recently. The topic was on the Fifth Step. During the discussion, a younger person in early

---

[3] *Twelve and Twelve*, at p. 68.
[4] *Twelve and Twelve*, at p. 97.

recovery rather excitedly shared that he had just finished his Fifth Step admissions with his sponsor and had decided to come to the meeting afterwards. He was obviously moved by the recent experience itself, as well as the coincidence that the meeting was on the Fifth Step. He shared, in a general way, about his making the admissions, how he was able to get to areas he had thought would remain secret, and the wonderful release he was still feeling as a result of the work just completed. As I sat and listened, I thought of the Eleventh Step, and the sharing I had recently heard in meetings, and knew what was troubling me. I simply changed the Steps: What if the topic had been on the Eleventh Step? Imagine hearing someone with equal enthusiasm share about just having finished a moving time of prayer and meditation before coming to the meeting. Then I imagined the person continuing to talk about what the experience had been like for him, and the areas of release he had felt. While it seems many of us can talk rather candidly of our direct experience with turning things over, writing inventories, and making admissions and amends, we seem reluctant to share our direct experience in prayer and meditation.

Why? Some simply have not developed a prayer and meditation practice of their own, and are not involved in any group that provides such a practice for its members.[5] Others seem to have dropped prayer and meditation as they have become busy about the affairs of life after recovery.[6] Bill W. himself may have fallen into this group: "I was astonished when I realized how little time I had actually been giving to my own elementary advice on meditation, prayer, and guidance – practices that I had so earnestly recommended to everybody else!"[7] And some do not believe in prayer and meditation and have found a way to remain sober without this practice.[8] "The other Steps can keep most of us sober and somehow functioning. But Step Eleven can keep us growing, if we try hard and work at it continually."[9]

---

[5] *Big Book*, at p. 87.
[6] *Twelve and Twelve*, at p. 96.
[7] *The Language of the Heart,* at p. 242.

[8] *Twelve and Twelve*, at pp. 96-97.
[9] *The Language of the Heart,* at p. 240.

The Spirituality of Sobriety

Finally, those of us who do have an Eleventh Step practice seem to be "shy on this matter of prayer," and just don't talk much about it in meetings.[10] The reluctance of this latter group may arise from some fear that to discuss these matters in a meeting would be proselytizing for their particular religion or group and would be inappropriate for an A.A. meeting. Others in this group, myself included to a degree, find compelling the following guidance often heard in meetings on the Higher Power: "There are just two things you need to know about God to make it in recovery. First, that there is one; and second, that you're not it!" The concept here is that in recovery we all find and relate to a "God as we understood Him." We pick up the bare form of a Higher Power in A.A. recovery; then we may find further detail in a particular religious organization or spiritual practice that we choose to join or follow. The result of that approach is that, in my experience, we do not often discuss our relationship with our Higher Power in our A.A. meetings.

Certainly, no one in recovery wants to attend an A.A. meeting and listen to someone preach on and on about the particulars of their own faith or religious denomination. None of this is going to help the people attending stay sober. After all, plenty of us now in recovery spent a great deal of our drinking careers remaining active in a religious denomination or faith! However, I do find of great interest the particulars of someone's practice in actual prayer and meditation. Not the doctrines and beliefs that may lay behind this, but just the practice itself. What are you doing in prayer, what are you doing in meditation? And then, what happens as a result? What is your direct experience in your times of prayer and meditation? This, I believe, is most appropriate sharing in an A.A. meeting on the Eleventh Step. Some share of a simple, but wise, practice learned from their sponsors: "I throw my car keys under the bed at night, and then when I wake in the morning, I have to get down on my knees to get them. While I am there, my sponsor told me to pray, 'God, help me get through today

---

[10] *Big Book*, at p. 85.

without a drink.'" This is quite appropriate sharing for an A.A. meeting. In fact, it often draws some laughs. But we should certainly not for a moment think lightly of this man's morning prayer practice. Otherwise we may quickly find ourselves in the situation like the Doctor of Theology who traveled to a deserted island to instruct in the proper form of prayer an ascetic hermit living there. The hermit did not even know the Lord's Prayer, so the good Doctor worked for days teaching it to him. Upon the Doctor's departure, when his boat was about a mile offshore, the hermit caught up with him – walking on the water – to ask him to repeat one of the lines of the prayer he had already forgotten! The Doctor of Theology realized his own foolishness and returned to the island to learn from the hermit. But what if a recovering alcoholic's prayer and meditation practice was more involved and more detailed than simply throwing keys under the bed at night? And what if the sharing included insight into the results of the particular practice? This would seem to be equally appropriate to share at an A.A. meeting. It is the same topic, just shared by someone with more experience in working the Eleventh Step.

We have a model for this provided in our literature. The Eleventh Step discussion in the *Twelve and Twelve* itself includes the Saint Francis prayer and a fairly detailed suggested form of meditation on that prayer in the Christian contemplative tradition.[11] Saint Francis is even acknowledged as not being an alcoholic, but nevertheless having given the world a prayer of such possible significance for the recovering alcoholic's prayer and meditation practice that it is specifically included and discussed in our literature. Is this the only prayer and form of meditation available to the recovering alcoholic? Absolutely not. This is only one; "the great men and women of all religions have left us a wonderful supply."[12] We are encouraged to go outside expressly authorized A.A. literature to find help and guidance in developing our Eleventh Step practice. If we have a specific religious or spiritual background, we are expressly encouraged to continue

---

[11] *Twelve and Twelve*, at pp. 99ff.
[12] *Twelve and Twelve*, at p. 99.

The Spirituality of Sobriety

that tradition: "If we belong to a religious denomination which requires a definite morning devotion, we attend to that also."[13] If we have left it behind, we are encouraged to return to it: "It is to be hoped that every A.A. who has a religious connection which emphasizes meditation will return to the practice of that devotion as never before."[14] If we have no particular religious tradition of our own, then it is suggested that we "select and memorize a few set prayers which emphasize the principles we have been discussing."[15]

We do not have to create a new prayer and meditation practice; we can freely borrow from others who have sought contact with God as they understood him through some form of prayer and meditation. "The actual experience of meditation and prayer across the centuries is, of course, immense. The world's libraries and places of worship are a treasure trove for all seekers."[16] Everything is open to us in developing our own approach to a meaningful Eleventh Step practice, and we are encouraged to seek help from religious and spiritual practitioners. "There are many helpful books also. Suggestions about these may be obtained from one's priest, minister, or rabbi. Be quick to see where religious people are right. Make use of what they offer."[17]

So what is this prayer and meditation practice as described in our A.A. literature? First, perhaps we should consider how our literature defines these terms. "Prayer and meditation are our principal means of conscious contact with God."[18] Prayer is defined as "a petition to God," and "the raising of the heart and mind to God."[19] Meditation may be thought of as included in prayer. Meditation is compared to constructive imagination, and is presented as a process in which we "envision our spiritual objective before we try to move toward it."[20] In meditation we "drop all resistance" to the subject of our meditation, and "rest quietly with the thoughts of someone who knows, so that we may experience and learn."[21] Meditation

---

[13] *Big Book*, at p. 87.
[14] *Twelve and Twelve*, at p. 98.
[15] *Big Book*, at p. 87.
[16] *Twelve and Twelve*, at p. 98.
[17] *Big Book*, at p. 87.

[18] *Twelve and Twelve*, at p. 96.
[19] *Twelve and Twelve*, at p. 102.
[20] *Twelve and Twelve*, at p. 100.
[21] *Twelve and Twelve*, at p. 100.

Prayer and Meditation in Recovery

as portrayed here should lead us to a learning on a more intuitive basis and to an actual experience that can be discussed with others.

The *Big Book* gives us "some definite and valuable suggestions" on a prayer practice.[22] At night before sleeping it is suggested that we review our behavior over the past day to identify areas of self-centeredness and other problems and where we might have done better. Then we proceed to a simple prayer to "ask God's forgiveness and inquire what corrective measures should be taken."[23] In the morning, before planning out our coming day, "we ask God to direct our thinking, especially asking that it be divorced from self-pity, dishonest or self-seeking motives."[24] As we then consider the plans for the day, if we are not sure of the appropriate direction at any point, "we ask God for inspiration, an intuitive thought or a decision. We relax and take it easy. We don't struggle."[25] The morning meditation is concluded with "a prayer that we be shown all through the day what our next step is to be, that we be given whatever we need to take care of such problems. We ask especially for freedom from self-will, and are careful to make no request for ourselves only."[26] We then follow a devotional practice from our own religious tradition, or "select and memorize a few set prayers which emphasize the principles we have been discussing."[27] Our morning meditation may be done alone, with our mate, or with friends. Then, during the course of the day, "we pause, when agitated or doubtful, and ask for the right thought or action. We constantly remind ourselves we are no longer running the show, humbly saying to ourselves many times each day 'Thy will be done.'"[28]

The *Twelve and Twelve* provides some additional suggestions for our prayer practice. We are cautioned that we should not "ask for specific solutions to specific problems, and for the ability to help other people as we have already thought they should be helped."[29] Petitions and requests of God in this form have an underlying presumption that we are still in charge

---

[22] *Big Book*, at p. 86.
[23] *Big Book*, at p. 86.
[24] *Big Book*, at p. 86.
[25] *Big Book*, at p. 86.
[26] *Big Book*, at p. 87.
[27] *Big Book*, at p, 87.
[28] *Big Book*, at pp. 87-88.
[29] *Twelve and Twelve*, at p. 102.

The Spirituality of Sobriety

and that we know how to fix things; it is me directing God to perform according to my will, instead of seeking God's will for the situation and the power to carry it out. This is the same Third Step issue making its appearance at a higher, more elevated level. But it is still self-centeredness, it is still me taking the part of the director instead of one of the actors in the play. A friend of mine related his experience at home when he fell into this presumptive form of prayer during the first year of his recovery. His wife informed him that not only was he still selfish and full of himself, but now he had a holier-than-thou attitude to go along with it! We are not seeking to glorify our own will in the course of our Eleventh Step work, but to find the will of our Higher Power in every situation in our lives. We ask for power to leave our own will behind as we carry out the will of our Higher Power as revealed.

During the course of the day, as we encounter times of great emotional disturbance, it is suggested that we "remember, and repeat to ourselves, a particular prayer or phrase that has appealed to us in our reading or meditation."[30] Many people in recovery memorize and use the Serenity Prayer for this purpose. In A.A. meetings we often use part of this prayer at the opening. I have found the entire prayer to be quite helpful for repetition during the more troubled parts of my day:

God, grant me the serenity to accept the things I cannot change,
The courage to change the things I can,
And the wisdom to know the difference.
Living one day at a time, enjoying one moment at a time,
Accepting hardship as a pathway to peace,
Taking this world as it is, not as I would have it,
Trusting that You will make all things right if I surrender to your will,
So that I may be reasonably happy in this life
And supremely happy with You forever in the next. Amen.

---

[30] *Twelve and Twelve,* at p. 103.

Other set prayers can also help slow us down and bring new, larger perspective to seemingly unresolvable pressing problems of the day. Sometimes I repeat the Third Step Prayer if it seems the difficulty is things not going my way for me, or the Seventh Step Prayer if I have the clarity of mind to see myself acting out a character defect in the situation. If I am totally overwhelmed in a situation that I cannot leave, then I have found the following prayer of dedication helpful to change my attitude back to usefulness and service:

> God, so draw my heart to you,
> So guide my mind,
> So fill my imagination,
> So control my will,
> That I may be wholly yours, utterly dedicated unto You;
> And then use me, I pray, as You will,
> And always to Your Glory and the welfare of Your people.

This kind of prayer practice right in the midst of my troubled times during the day often restores emotional balance, brings some clarity and new perspective to the situation, and brings me back to God's will instead of the pursuit of my own will in the situation.

But it is not always so easy to engage in prayer. Sometimes it is simply the practice. "All of us, without exception, pass through times when we can pray only with the greatest exertion of will."[31] So prayer, also, may be a place where we may need to exercise our willpower in parallel with God's will. In my own experience, I have had many times where prayer felt like trying to open a gate frozen up on rusty hinges – lots of creaking and groaning, but not much actual opening of the gate. The *Twelve and Twelve* suggests we "simply resume prayer as soon as we can, doing what we know to be good for us."[32] There are times for me when I continue with the prayer because of a deep sense of things about God needing to be said by a

---

[31] *Twelve and Twelve*, at p. 105.
[32] *Twelve and Twelve*, at p. 105.

human being; that the words themselves, spoken with intent if not with feeling, will release energy and create change. However, prayer does become meaningless to the extent it has become rote and repetitive for its own sake:

> This act is prayer, by which term I understand no vain exercise of words, no mere repetition of certain sacred formulae, but the very movement itself of the soul, putting itself in a personal relation of contact with the mysterious power of which it feels the presence, — it may be even before it has a name by which to call it. Wherever this interior prayer is lacking, there is no religion; wherever, on the other hand, this prayer rises and stirs the soul, even in the absence of forms or of doctrines, we have living religion.[33]

While the efficacy of my prayer on any given day is not based on my particular feelings of inspiration on that day, there is a need for true prayer to have this "interior" feel to it and not be mere form.

The *Twelve and Twelve* contains a more detailed approach to meditation for the beginner. As an example of a method, we are first presented with the Saint Francis prayer, and it is suggested that we "reread this prayer several times very slowly, savoring every word and trying to take in the deep meaning of each phrase and idea."[34] We then "relax and breathe deeply of the spiritual atmosphere with which the grace of this prayer surrounds us."[35] We are trying to touch something beyond the words, to get to the thought and the feeling associated with the words, to more fully understand what is being said in the text in a more intuitive manner with more spiritual awareness. We then engage in something like constructive imagination to read the prayer again and "try to see what its inner essence is."[36] We spend some time considering the words of the

---

[33] William James, *The Varieties of Religious Experience* (New York: Penguin Books, 1958), at p. 352.

[34] *Twelve and Twelve*, at p. 99.
[35] *Twelve and Twelve*, at p. 100.
[36] *Twelve and Twelve*, at p. 101.

prayer from many different perspectives, always open to fresh thoughts and feelings arising from the continuous looking deeply. If negative thoughts break in, we quietly move away from them and move back toward the subject of the meditation.[37]

This form of meditation outlined in the *Twelve and Twelve* follows a Christian contemplative tradition. Other forms of meditation have been introduced to Westerners in more recent years from Hindu and Buddhist sources, particularly from yoga, Zen and Tibetan Buddhism. The mystical elements of Christianity, Judaism and Islam all have centering, contemplative, and meditative practices. Many of these forms of meditation work on quieting the activity of the mind rather than focusing thought on a particular subject. The meditation is more a time of allowing all thoughts to recede, with perhaps a focus of attention only on the in and out of the breath. Some practices include the chanting of a mantra such as "Ommm…." Some teach a mindfulness practice of looking deeply at areas of our lives. One spiritual teacher has defined meditation as "the experience of who we are other than our thoughts." As our thoughts quiet, we begin to see a sense of self at a deeper level than the concept presented by the mind's more frantic thinking about ourselves.

I have been working a Sufi practice recently that involves the quieting of the thoughts and then a moving of awareness to the heart with a focus of attention on opening the heart more. While my mind may never understand God, I do believe that my heart is capable of loving Him. "Though we cannot know him we can love him. By love he may be touched and embraced, never by thought."[38] Just as we find we know better the person we love, I am finding improved conscious contact with God as I work to open my heart more toward Him and all His creation.

Our Eleventh Step meditation practice is wide open, has no boundaries, and can always be further developed. Our practice is to be "[a]ided by such instruction and example as we can find," and "it is

---

[37] *Twelve and Twelve*, at p. 100.
[38] William Johnson, ed., *The Cloud of Unknowing* (New York: Doubleday, 1973), at p. 54.

essentially an individual adventure, something which each one of us works out in his own way."[39] We are invited to seek out further instruction and practice in any spiritual tradition we may choose. We are cautioned that our meditation practice should always have as its object "to improve our conscious contact with God, with His grace, wisdom, and love."[40]

And there we have the outline of a prayer and meditation practice that should prove acceptable to almost anyone. The form of daily times of devotion, and some general subject areas for both prayer and meditation are provided. But the content is left wide open for each practitioner to fill in herself in the course of her own discoveries. We are encouraged to seek help and instruction from previous religious connections, other spiritual traditions that we may find meaningful, and to obtain further instruction and suggestions in both prayer and meditation from "helpful books" as well as others who can teach us. While our prayer and meditation practice may come to be done individually, with family or friends, or in some religious or spiritual group outside of A.A., the real-life experience we receive of the improvement of our conscious contact with God, coming to know God's will for us, and the provisioning of the power to carry it out in our lives, as well as the feelings, thoughts, and changes in attitudes, relationships and situations that result, are all things to be shared with our fellow-A.A.'s in the expansive context of the Eleventh Step.

[39] *Twelve and Twelve*, at p. 101.
[40] *Twelve and Twelve*, at p. 101.

Chapter 13

Improving our Conscious Contact with God

"... to improve our conscious contact with God as we understood Him...."

Step Eleven

The Eleventh Step is not where we first meet our Higher Power. If not in the First Step itself, we certainly encountered Him in some way at the Second Step, and in the Third Step we turned everything over to Him. Step Five may have been where we "first actually felt the presence of God."[1] And our work at Step Seven results in a profound "change in our attitude toward God."[2] The Eleventh Step is where we begin to work at improving our conscious contact with this God as we have come to understand Him. Up to now, our encounters with our Higher Power have been in the course of working the program of recovery, and receiving help from Him as we went along. Now we begin the work of getting to know better our Higher Power. The tools we use for this work are prayer and meditation, just like those of most religions and spiritual traditions.

"Prayer and meditation are our principal means of conscious contact with God."[3] It is to make this conscious contact that the alcoholic in

---

[1] Twelve and Twelve, at p. 62.
[2] Twelve and Twelve, at p. 75.
[3] Twelve and Twelve, at p. 96.

recovery is praying and meditating. We do not take on this practice for the sole reason that our particular religious affiliation requires or expects this of its members. We do not learn a meditation practice in order to relieve stress and improve our health and outlook. We do not go to prayer because we feel "called to God" as the result of some conversion experience. All these are certainly benefits of the practice and good reasons in themselves for taking on prayer and meditation. However, as recovering alcoholics, we are engaged in this practice for the very specific purpose of "improving our conscious contact with God as we understood Him."

I have found this conscious contact to consist of a simple heightened awareness, a mindfulness similar to Buddhist practice. It seems to me to come in expanded thought and feeling. The picture I sometimes see is of a vast reservoir constituting Carl Jung's unconscious into which I have submerged countless memories, feelings, desires, and dreams. In the course of prayer and meditation, the sense of a loving presence and acceptance allows these submerged materials to float to the surface, coming into my conscious awareness. But it is a deeper level of work that seems to me to then bring the improved conscious contact with God. This is a sense of the rigid boundary between my limited conscious awareness and this vast unconscious reservoir softening and becoming more permeable to a flow from the depths to the surface. I think of the depths of this unconsciousness as my higher self, my spiritual connection, or God within me, and the flow moving from it as the improved conscious contact with God.

I do not always have feelings associated with this sense of the flow of God's presence into my life, but often I do. While this may sound a bit too mystical, I have found it to be quite simple. In my Second Step, I acquired a belief in a Higher Power capable of encountering me in such a way that this Higher Power could actually help me with my problem. This belief in a Higher Power grew exponentially during the course of my work in the Steps as a result of what I experienced. I do not find it a bit unusual that when

Improving our Conscious Contact with God

this Higher Power is presented to my consciousness by way of the belief I have developed that I actually have an emotional response.

When I lived in South Florida, I often hiked in the everglades. It was not unusual to come upon a snake in the trail. While the snake slithered off into the marsh or bush, it always gave me a startle, if not more of a shock. Sometimes, though, what I thought was a snake was only a stick laying in the trail. This happened so frequently we called it the "Florida Stick Snake." I would have the same emotional response when I mistook the stick for a snake as I did when it was really a snake. In other words, if I believed a stick was a snake and presented it as such to my consciousness, I had an emotional response based on that belief, regardless of any objective reality. I find a similar process at work when I believe my Higher Power present in my life and I present Him to my consciousness in the course of prayer and meditation. The perception comes by faith rather than through a physical sense organ. This does not seem to divorce it from my feelings. So, this improved conscious contact with God, for me, comes as an expansion of thought and feeling.

As we continue in our prayer and meditation practice, and this conscious contact is made, things begin to happen. The results of our Eleventh Step practice are not matters of faith and belief; rather, they are "matters of knowledge and experience."[4] After even a short time working with prayer and meditation, "unexpected results followed, we felt different; in fact we *knew* different."[5] The profound changes resulting from our inventories, admissions, and amends, become the real-life experiences that we share with others in regard to our earlier work in the Steps. In a similar manner, the profound changes resulting from our prayer and meditation practice become real-life experiences that can be shared in regard to our Eleventh Step work.

Looking back from the perspective of the Eleventh Step, the previous work in the Steps appears as a continuum leading to prayer and meditation.

---

[4] Twelve and Twelve, at p. 104.
[5] Twelve and Twelve, at p. 97.

The Spirituality of Sobriety

"There is a direct linkage among self-examination, meditation, and prayer."[6] The self-examination involved in all the earlier Steps, but particularly Steps Four through Ten, focuses rather dramatically upon "the dark and negative side of our natures."[7] Some in recovery suggest including the good things about ourselves in our Fourth Step inventories as well, sort of a balance sheet approach of both assets and liabilities. However, for me, it was my work in the Eleventh Step that brought me into contact with the better parts of me, the parts I now think of as my "higher self." It is in prayer and meditation that "the good that is in us all, even in the worst of us," flowers and grows.[8] Meditation is the opening to sunlight that feeds the growth of the good within us. While my mind is clearing in recovery, my emotions are coming into some balance and the promise concerning intuitive knowing is beginning to occur, I come to find in the course of developing my Eleventh Step practice that it is prayer and meditation that are providing "vitally needed support" to my mind, emotions and intuition for their continued development.[9]

The sense of a higher self, and an identification of this sense with a Higher Power exterior to ourselves, followed by a movement away from the limited self and a growing connection to this higher self, forms the "common nucleus" underlying the particular creeds and beliefs of all religions. William James, in his work, *The Varieties of Religious Experience*, that greatly influenced Bill Wilson's thinking and writings, traces the development of this sense of the higher self:

> The individual, so far as he suffers from his wrongness and criticises it, is to that extent consciously beyond it, and in at least possible touch with something higher, if anything higher exist. Along with the wrong part there is thus a better part of him, even though it may be but a most helpless germ.[10]

---

[6] Twelve and Twelve, at p. 98.
[7] Twelve and Twelve, at p. 98.
[8] Twelve and Twelve, at p. 98.
[9] Twelve and Twelve, at p. 97.

[10] William James, The Varieties of Religious Experience (New York: Penguin Group, 1958), at p. 383.

Improving our Conscious Contact with God

James then summarizes the movement of our sense of connection to this higher self that is reflected in all religious activity:

> They allow for the divided self and the struggle; they involve the change of personal center and the surrender of the lower self; they express the appearance of exteriority of the helping power and yet account for our sense of union with it.[11]

It would seem that my spiritual experience of movement of the identification of my sense of self from a lower to a higher self, and then the union of that higher self with a power outside myself, is the essence of all religious work.

And it is in the continuing development of my mind, emotions and intuition that I begin to see the fruits of my improved conscious contact with my Higher Power. While we begin to gain some emotional balance in Step Ten, we get additional help in Step Eleven. "One of [meditation's] first fruits is emotional balance."[12] In meditation, I slow things down and create space around feelings clamoring to be heard; I allow each feeling to present itself and deliver its message. But in meditation I am able to avoid attaching to any one of them. The emotion becomes like water flowing through me, and meditation is the lifting of the dam to allow each emotion to continue its flow without attachment to me so that the next feeling has its own space to flow through me as it arises. Instead of ignoring the feeling, or stuffing it, I can give it appropriate attention in meditation, thank it for showing up, and then allow it to move on without attaching to it. Meditation takes me out of the analysis and rationalization of my feelings, and moves me to synthesis and higher awareness, where each feeling is given its due respect, but none are permitted to take over and run the whole show. As a result of this work, I begin to find my full range of emotions, a spectrum of color I did not know I had, and they all begin to come into balance with each other and the particular situation at hand.

---

[11] The Varieties of Religious Experience, at p. 384.
[12] Twelve and Twelve, at pp. 101-102.

The Spirituality of Sobriety

Equally profound changes begin to occur in my mind as a result of my Eleventh Step practice. "Our thought-life will be placed on a much higher plane."[13] Sometimes we hear someone say in A.A. meetings, "My best thinking got me here." This assertion is generally followed up with statements about keeping the program simple and not over-intellectualizing an otherwise simple program. While there is certainly some good recovery wisdom in all this, it also seems to me an indication that the person has not yet worked this Eleventh Step. In the course of our prayer and meditation practice, "we ask God to direct our thinking."[14] As a result, we find that "we can employ our mental faculties with assurance, for after all God gave us brains to use."[15] I was professionally trained as an attorney, graduating at the top of my class and working for a top law firm building a successful (before the drinking went out of hand!) career based on top-quality rational thinking. But I can honestly say today that I never achieved my "best thinking" until after I had worked my way through the Steps and had developed a strong Eleventh Step practice.

The very nature of my thinking changes in the course of continued recovery. In my prayer practice, I actively seek from God "inspiration, an intuitive thought."[16] And I begin to find them! "What used to be the hunch or the occasional inspiration gradually becomes a working part of the mind."[17] I move from so much analysis and breaking things down into individual pieces, to more synthesis and building things into new and more meaningful relationships. My "inspired" thinking becomes more open and creative, less closed and rational. New understandings are welcomed and encouraged. My conclusions are now seen as the result of a selective attribution of significance to certain facts pulled from the general field based on my own internal judgment of importance. Now, in meditation, more facts are allowed to move from the background field into a place of significance causing a rearrangement of focus and new perceptions not possible through old analysis and rationalism. We "find that our thinking

---

[13] Big Book, at p. 86.
[14] Big Book, at p. 86.
[15] Big Book, at p. 86.

[16] Big Book, at p. 86.
[17] Big Book, at p. 87.

will, as time passes, be more and more on the plane of inspiration. We come to rely upon it."[18]

The very first attempts at meditation revealed to me much about the working of my mind. As I sat quietly resting my awareness just on my breaths in and out, I remember how amazed I was at how incredibly difficult this was to maintain. My awareness was almost immediately distracted by incessant thoughts about trivial matters that took on seemingly great importance. I became aware of how busy and noisy my mind was even when at rest. This, of course, is the ego-mind demanding attention for itself. With all this noise and distraction going on in my mind, I began to see why it is often so difficult to really understand what another person is saying. Suddenly, any meaningful communication between people began to look miraculous given the distraction taking place in our minds while we are talking and listening. With the busy ego-mind fully engaged all the time, I saw how impossible it would be to develop the capacity to hear the inspiration or intuitive thought from God. I first must quiet the mind to open the channel for the intuition and inspiration. Meditation became the means to relieve the internal chatter and distraction. Over time, with repeated practice, I was able to bring quiet to my mind and maintain a focus merely on the breath. With continued practice, even during my normal daytime activities, I have found space developing between the thoughts where they used to run in tight formation like train cars linked together. In this space, there is now room for an intuitive thought or inspiration to find its way into my otherwise busy mind.

We also develop a deep sense of belonging in the course of our Eleventh Step work. In Step Five we found relief from "that terrible sense of isolation," and gained "the sense of belonging," as we made our admissions and connected with another human being at the deep places in our lives.[19] "Step Five .... was the beginning of true kinship with man and God."[20] That sense of belonging, begun in relationship to another human

---

[18] Big Book, at p. 87.
[19] Twelve and Twelve, at p. 57.
[20] Twelve and Twelve, at p. 57.

The Spirituality of Sobriety

being in the course of our Fifth Step admissions, now comes into full focus in relationship to God in the course of our Eleventh Step work. "Perhaps one of the greatest rewards of meditation and prayer is the sense of *belonging* that comes to us. We no longer live in a completely hostile world. We are no longer lost and frightened and purposeless."[21]

Where I used to see the universe as working against me, requiring me to independently manage things to my own best advantage in order to try to succeed at life, I now find myself more in a synchronous relationship with the universe, with my own interests naturally flowing into larger interests around me. I cease pushing my own small interests and find myself more drawn to those larger interests, becoming part of something bigger than myself. It is a continuation of the Third Step work where "we became less and less interested in ourselves, our little plans and designs. More and more we became interested in seeing what we could contribute to life."[22] I find myself fitting more comfortably into the flow around me.

While we may, at first, think this focus on prayer and meditation way too "out there" for the recovering alcoholic, as the fruits of the Eleventh Step practice begin to show up, we find that the Eleventh Step is "in reality intensely practical."[23] In addition to the emotional balance and inspired thinking, we also "become much more efficient."[24] When people talk to me about their difficulties in finding time in their busy schedule for prayer and meditation, my response often is that I don't have enough time in the day not to pray and meditate! The efficiency that I have found in my ability to move through work and life issues, to reach good decisions quickly, to do or say something right the first time, as a result of my Eleventh Step practice has completely sold me on the necessity of prayer and meditation for a full and effective sober life. The Eleventh Step is the point where life finally becomes easier, more fun. "We relax and take it easy. We don't struggle."[25] And I find new energy available to more completely give myself to family, friends, work and service. "We do not tire so easily, for we are

---

[21] Twelve and Twelve, at p. 105.
[22] Big Book, at p. 63.
[23] Twelve and Twelve, at p. 101.

[24] Big Book, at p. 88.
[25] Big Book, at p. 86.

not burning up energy foolishly as we did when we were trying to arrange life to suit ourselves."[26] We see with more clarity, our emotions are lighter and flowing, our thinking is intuitive and inspired, and we find that deep sense of belonging to the world around us. "Intensely practical?"[27] You bet.

---

[26] Big Book, at p. 88.
[27] Twelve and Twelve, at p. 101.

Chapter 14
Knowledge of His Will
for Us

"... praying only for knowledge
of His will for us..."

Step Eleven

Having developed a prayer and meditation practice, and gained a
conscious contact with God, we are now directed by the last part of the
Eleventh Step to pray "only for knowledge of His will for us and the power
to carry that out." Early in recovery, as I began to develop a short morning
devotional practice, I had no idea what this meant. I thought perhaps I was
going to receive mystical solutions to all the legal, financial, family and job
problems confronting me at the end of my drinking career. But that is not
the way it works. I still remember getting the message one morning during
my devotional time that God's will for me was real simple – stay sober and
start working the Steps! I was to get through the rest of the day without
drinking, find my way to an A.A. meeting that night, and start reading and
talking to people about Step One. The sort of vision I had of this at the time
was having jumped forward to the Eleventh Step, and finding that its
direction was to go full circle back to Step One. And I still believe the truth
of that message to this day. As I continue to bring my life into accord with
the principles of the Twelve Steps, I find I am also lined up with God's will
for me that day.[1] Nothing ever did come through the astroplane about all
those other problems, but they did work themselves out over time.

---

[1] *Twelve and Twelve*, at p. 40.

The Spirituality of Sobriety

Following those early days in recovery, I pursued a knowledge of God's will for me as if it were something objective to search for among all the other things out there, and that the tools to use for this search were prayer and meditation. I was thinking of God's will as independent information available to me if I could just find it. It was as though I were looking for the directions so I could figure out how to run some complicated electronic device. Or, as if God's will would be independent counsel with God acting the part of an advisor or consultant providing me with His opinion which I could then compare with other opinions, and my own will, and then make a choice as to which opinion I would accept and follow for that particular issue. I would pray and I would meditate, but nothing came.

I did tap into guidance from God's will in this sort of objective way over the years in a limited amount. Looking back, I can easily see God's will in many specific things my sponsors have suggested and shared with me. Much of their guidance for me as I was working my way through what seemed at the time to be very complicated and difficult issues, I can now see as divinely inspired. I have also received knowledge of God's will for me from others in recovery in the course of sharing our lives and experience with each other. This guidance sometimes comes in the form of direct suggestions for what I might do or, more often, as people simply share with me related experiences from their own life in dealing with an issue like mine. This more objective form of guidance also comes to me routinely as I attend A.A. meetings. As I hear the experience of others in the course of their sharing pieces of their own stories, and those pieces come into relation with my own life, I often receive guidance that I know is God's will for me.

Knowledge of God's will for me arriving in this more objective form of assistance, guidance, and suggestions from others is like the story told in A.A. meetings of the man trapped on the roof of his house in a flood and praying to God to rescue him. Someone comes by in a boat, but the man declines help since he has prayed and is believing that God will rescue him. Another comes in a helicopter, but the man declines again, remaining

Knowledge of His Will for Us

strong in his faith that God will rescue him. Finally, he drowns and, finding himself in heaven, asks God why He didn't answer his prayer and rescue him from the flood. God responds, "Well, I sent one of my servants in a boat to get you, and then I sent another in a helicopter, but they said you wouldn't come!" Often, the knowledge of God's will for me comes to me through the words and experiences of others. The help and guidance is there as long as I do not get distracted about the particular form in which it shows up.

However, receiving knowledge of God's will for me in this more objective form from other people became cumbersome for everyday living. Obviously, it is impossible to check in with someone else every time before saying or doing anything. I began to focus a lot of attention on the *Big Book's* promise that we "will intuitively know how to handle situations which used to baffle us."[2] I wanted very much for this promise to come true in my life. As I read in the A.A. literature of receiving inspiration and guidance as discussed in Chapter 13, and of having that kind of inspiration become "a working part of the mind,"[3] I became more frustrated with my own lack of intuitive thinking. I continued for some time in prayer and meditation seeking this kind of inspiration and actively praying for knowledge of His will for me. However, the direct inspiration and intuitive thinking I was seeking continued to elude me. After some time, I began to realize I had no more idea what God's will was for me than I did before I started praying and meditating. What was I doing wrong?

More recently, I have come to see the problem for me was the need for more Third Step work. I was still running on the power of self-will, I was just looking to God for the direction to move in. If God would just issue the orders, then I would move out and make it happen! This was how I received knowledge of God's will in the more objective form from my sponsor and others: they would make suggestions or share their own experience, and I would then implement the suggestion in my own life

[2] *Big Book*, at p. 84.
[3] *Big Book*, at p. 87.

147

situation. Why would it not continue to work this way, but with my receiving the directions directly from God as inspiration?

As I continued to seek direct inspiration of the knowledge of God's will for my life, I began to find my perspective on God's will slowly changing. I began to see its essence as simply the alternative to my own self-will. Then I started seeing this contrast of God's will to my will showing up in the literature, some places even seeming to emphasize the contrast between the two. The Step Eleven discussion in the *Twelve and Twelve* suggests the best way to get back to emotional balance is "our search for God's will, not our own, in the moment of stress."[4] The *Big Book* suggests the following thought go with us all through the day in order to maintain our spiritual condition: "Thy will (not mine) be done."[5] Similarly, the *Twelve and Twelve* contrasts "self-determined objectives" with "the perfect objective which is of God," and expressly contrasts our own "limited objectives" with "God's will for us."[6]

With the understanding of this very tight contrasting relationship between my own self-will, which had been the focus of my work in the Third Step, and God's will which I was now seeking in the Eleventh Step, I could see that the prayer for knowledge of God's will for me was the completion of the work I started with the decision I made in the Third Step. There I made the decision to stop acting out of my own self-will. But I had not yet come to understand how to find an alternative basis for making everyday decisions in my life. I had made the decision *not* to do my own self-will, but had not obtained the direct knowledge of God's will to know what to do and say in day-to-day life. I was relying on sponsors and others for guidance, but had not yet made the direct connection to the inspiration and had not developed the intuitive thinking that would open me more to God's will.

The first step, for me, was to stop all the self-will. I could divide my life into two major parts along the lines of the Serenity Prayer – the things

---

[4] *Twelve and Twelve*, at p. 103.
[5] *Big Book*, at p. 85.
[6] *Twelve and Twelve*, at pp. 68-69.

happening around me that I could not change, and the things that I could change. With acceptance as the key to those things I could not change, the more passive aspect of the Third Step was already helping me to refrain from acting out of my own self-will. As I accepted the things I could not change, I did come to see these things as God's will at that time. I connected strongly with some wisdom from Meister Eckhart, the great medieval Christian mystic:

> You might ask, "How can I know if something is God's will?" My answer is, "if it were not God's will, it wouldn't exist even for an instant; so if something happens, it *must* be his will." If you truly enjoyed God's will, you would feel exactly as though you were in the kingdom of heaven, whatever happened to you or didn't happen to you.[7]

I could do this fairly early in recovery because not much in the way of action was required; rather, the work was to accept what was happening without seeking to change it. The work was internal to me — to change attitudes inside so that I could deeply and sincerely accept without rancor.

It was with the things I could change that I was having the difficulties. Here, I needed knowledge of some will other than my own if I was to avoid acting out of my own self-will; and this was the knowledge that was lacking. I began to see that the problem was in my conception of God's will as something independent of me, as some objective message that I could hear and then decide to follow or not. I did not yet have "a desire to seek *and do* God's will" as a basic ingredient of the humility I was learning in the course of my Seventh Step work.[8] My attitude toward the doing of God's will was wrong, and my perception of the nature of God's will was wrong. Other spiritual teachers seemed to agree with this assessment of my condition: "If you were truly humble you would not bother about yourself at all. Why should you? You would only be concerned with God and with His will and

---

[7] Quoted in Stephen Mitchell, *The Gospel According to Jesus* (New York: HarperCollins, 1991), at p. 177.
[8] *Twelve and Twelve*, at p. 72.

The Spirituality of Sobriety

with the objective order of things and values as they are, and not as your selfishness wants them to be."[9] I was still more apt to tell God what His will should be than to simply and sincerely ask what it was for me.[10] No wonder I had no intuitive knowledge of God's will for me. "We discover that we do receive guidance for our lives to just about the extent that we stop making demands upon God to give it to us on order on our terms."[11] I still had more basic work to do.

Then the revelation. I had not yet really turned over my will to the care of God. I was still hanging on to it, and then comparing it to God's will, as if they were alternative choices instead of two parallel things in agreement with each other, heading in the same direction simultaneously. "It is when we try to make our will conform to God's that we begin to use it rightly. To all of us, this was a most wonderful revelation."[12] It certainly was for me. If we are carrying a desire for God's will with us through the day, then "[w]e can exercise our will power along this line all we wish. It is the proper use of the will."[13] The Sufis have a wonderful picture of this relationship between our will and God's will:

> Consider your will as being like the branch of a tree, and the divine will to be the whole tree. Instead of thinking that your will is a certain will and the divine will is another will, look at it as one tree. Then, somehow, you can call upon a level of your being which you do not limit to your individual ego, and which will give you much more power.[14]

Then I had a dream that brought all this into clarity for me. In the dream, I am a ten year old boy in the garage at the workbench in my home with an electric power saw in my hands. I am not cutting any wood with the saw, and do not really know what to do with it. I am just waving it around with the power on and the cutting blade spinning. A voice-over in the dream

---

[9] Thomas Merton, *New Seeds of Contemplation,* at page 189.
[10] *Twelve and Twelve,* at p. 31.
[11] *Twelve and Twelve,* at p. 104.
[12] *Twelve and Twelve*, at p. 40.

[13] *Big Book*, at p. 85.
[14] Pir Vilayat Inayat Khan, *That Which Transpires Behind That Which Appears* (New Lebanon, NY: Omega Publications, 1994), at p. 119.

suggested that I should simply set the saw down, just lay it down on the floor. The understanding I was receiving at the same time was that there was nothing wrong with the saw. The problem was it was much too powerful a tool for me to handle without my father's direction. It was my own independent use of the power saw that threatened harm to others as well as myself. However, if I used it in parallel with the direction of my father, then the power saw would not hurt others or me. The power saw was my will, and my father's direction would become God's will for me. With these two in agreement, a lot of work could get done and no one would get hurt. My own independent use of the will endangered everyone around, including myself, and would not accomplish any work. *"Our whole trouble had been the misuse of willpower. We had tried to bombard our problems with it instead of attempting to bring it into agreement with God's intention for us."*[15]

Now I could understand how I could turn my will over to God in the Third Step, and at the same time be told that "[a]ll of the Twelve Steps require sustained and personal exertion to conform to their principles."[16] After having turned my will over to God in the Third Step, I was confused how the Fifth Step could then tell me: "No one ought to say the A.A. program requires no willpower; here is one place you may require all you've got."[17] Now I could see that the turning over of my will was not as an alternative to some objective and opposite will of God, but rather was a laying down of my will so as to bring it into agreement with God's. I was to lay the power saw down so that I could learn to properly use it under the direction of my father. I got another picture of this relationship while playing tennis. If my swing is just the arm and hand holding the racquet, there is little power and I am likely to injure tendons and the weaker parts of the arm and joints. However, if my swing includes my much stronger abdominal muscles in a twisting and my big leg muscles in a bending and lunging, then I have much more power in the stroke and am less likely to

---

[15] *Twelve and Twelve*, at p. 40.
[16] *Twelve and Twelve*, at p. 40.
[17] *Twelve and Twelve*, at p. 61.

injure the arm. I now see my will as the arm and hand, and God's will as the bigger, stronger muscles of the abdomen and legs in the tennis stroke. If all are functioning together, the result is a sharply hit return with pace, and no injuries. And so now I was ready, both in my perception of God's will and my attitude toward the doing of it, for the inspiration to begin coming.

In my new state of perception and attitude, I could see that God's will for me was not contrary to our instinctual needs, but rather that His will covered "the whole range of our needs."[18] Seeking appropriate satisfaction of our instinctual needs would not be inconsistent with God's will, but would rather be quite in agreement with His will for me. "We are sure God wants us to be happy, joyous, and free."[19] As I began my work on the last part of the Twelfth Step, with its radical change in approach to the instincts as we practice the principles of the Twelve Steps in all our affairs after our spiritual awakening, it became quite clear to me that my normal everyday activities surrounding the appropriate satisfaction of my instinctual needs would place me clearly in God's will. There need not be any conflict here.

I have also found a whole new level of acceptance flowing in my life now. My new perception and attitude toward God's will has me welcoming people and events into my life on a whole new basis. It is no longer a grudging acceptance of certain less-than-desired people and events that come into my life. "'God's will' is certainly found in anything that is required of us in order that we may be united with one another in love."[20] Now, I often can see right past the person or event to the One who is responsible for bringing this person or event into my life at just this moment. I receive what comes, not as from the person or event, but as from the One who gave it. The assumption then becomes that everything showing up in my life comes as the will of God for me at that time. However, my response may be to seek courage to change what showed up, and I may actively work to remove this same thing from my life. But its

---

[18] *Twelve and Twelve*, at p. 102.
[19] *Big Book*, at p. 133.
[20] *New Seeds of Contemplation*, at p. 76.

initial showing up is only by the will of God for me at that moment. The fact that someone shows up in my life today, and that I acknowledge God as the one responsible for bringing this person into my life, does not necessarily mean that I should not seek courage to remove the person from my life so that he is not in my life tomorrow! The significance of anything or anyone showing up in my life today always includes the opportunity for spiritual growth and the continued practice of the principles in all my affairs, including this one.

The direct inspiration did begin to come. The promise came true. "We realize we know only a little. God will constantly disclose more to you and to us. Ask Him in your morning meditation what you can do each day for the man who is still sick. The answers will come...."[21] I often find myself intuitively handling a situation arising today that would have baffled me before. It's easy. That sort of inspiration has now become "a working part of the mind," and I have "come to rely upon it."[22] I find myself responding to situations both at work and at home in ways that, upon later reflection, sometimes blows me away. That I had acted under some inspiration from a source outside myself is sometimes so clear to me because of my knowledge from my Fourth Step inventories of how I have acted on my own in the past. When I am stumped and have no idea how to proceed, or have multiple choices available but no clear direction, I now "ask God for inspiration."[23] And answers often come.

Having received some specific guidance, I still find it most helpful to check it out with my sponsor, my spiritual advisor, and/or my family and friends depending upon the specific issue. I take to heart the *Big Book's* caution: "it is not probable that we are going to be inspired at all times. We might pay for this presumption in all sorts of absurd actions and ideas."[24] If my deepest desire in the situation is to align my will with God's will and work for "the perfect objective which is of God," then I find it quite natural to check in with others on the guidance I feel I have received.[25] On the

---

[21] *Big Book,* at p. 164.
[22] *Big Book*, at p. 87.
[23] *Big Book*, at p. 86.

[24] *Big Book*, at p. 87.
[25] *Twelve and Twelve*, at p. 68.

153

other hand, if my deepest desire in the situation is to do what I feel the guidance is directing, then I find myself wanting to resist running the guidance by others for a reality check. I am afraid someone may suggest I should wait for more clarity, and that I will not be able to do what, in reality, is my own desire masquerading as God's will. The *Twelve and Twelve* describes just such a man, and concludes: "With the best of intentions, he tends to force his own will into all sorts of situations and problems with the comfortable assurance that he is acting under God's specific direction. Under such an illusion, he can of course create great havoc without in the least intending it."[26] It always remains possible that the guidance I think I have received by inspiration as knowledge of God's will is nothing more than "well-intentioned unconscious rationalizations."[27] Checking in with trusted others who know me is the best way I have found to prevent this from happening.

Finally, we should note that our prayer for knowledge of God's will is for us, not for others. We are not directed to pray for knowledge of God's will for other people. Each person should be making this prayer for himself. Our prayers requesting specific things for other people "are fundamentally good acts, but often they are based upon a supposition that we know God's will for the person for whom we pray. This means that side by side with an earnest prayer there can be a certain amount of presumption and conceit in us."[28] To avoid this presumption and conceit, it is suggested that any such prayer for another person include the simple request for God's will, whatever that may be. We may pray for a specific problem, but we should not presume to demand of God any specific solution as His will. I find it most helpful to make my requests known, but then leave the method of solution with God. I am constrained by my mind, but with God the possible array of solutions is endless. Why should I limit what may be the best solution?

---

[26] *Twelve and Twelve*, at p. 104.
[27] *Twelve and Twelve*, at p. 103.
[28] *Twelve and Twelve*, at p. 104.

Knowledge of His Will for Us

The self-centeredness and egocentricity is so strong and pervasive in my life that it can even take over the prayer and meditation practice of the Eleventh Step! It seems my ego does not care so much what I am doing, as long as it is in control of the doing. Prayer and meditation is ok, as long as it is still the "I" doing it. Other spiritual writers have seen this issue, and noted that self-will is still self-will, and that if my selfish desires

> reach out for the good things of the interior life, for recollection, for peace, for the pleasures of prayer, if they are no more than the natural and selfish desires they will make recollection difficult and even impossible.... If you give up all these desires and seek one thing only, God's will, he will give you recollection and peace in the middle of labor and conflict and trial.[29]

There is great wisdom in our Eleventh Step direction to keep our prayer practice closely focused on the knowledge of God's will for us. This, itself, helps keep in check my egocentricity and protects the prayer and meditation practice from being hijacked by my self-centeredness.

What seemed to be a simple prayer request for knowledge of God's will for me became the method of completing the work begun in the Third Step of moving out of the self-centeredness and self-will that was the "root of our troubles."[30] I now had the knowledge of God's will as an alternative for my old self-will. And then I found that the turning over of my will to God was only to bring it into accord with His will so that I could exercise my will properly. Today, I find this congruence of my will and God's will working together in the service work I do and in my continued practice of the principles in all my affairs.

The *Twelve and Twelve* suggests an experiential result of gaining some knowledge of God's will for us: "The moment we catch even a glimpse of God's will, the moment we begin to see truth, justice, and love as the real and eternal things in life, we are no longer deeply disturbed by all the

---

[29] *New Seeds of Contemplation,* at pp. 207-208.
[30] *Big Book*, at p. 62.

seeming evidence to the contrary that surrounds us in purely human affairs."[31] With knowledge of God's will growing, I find myself connected more with this bigger picture of what God is doing in His world, and less connected with this world as seen in terms of the "purely human affairs." There is now something greater, of more significance, and infinitely more meaningful to me, behind every person and event that I encounter in the course of my day-to-day living.

[31] *Twelve and Twelve,* at p. 105.

Chapter 15
The Power

"... and the power to carry that out."

Step Eleven

The alcoholic finds herself confronted with personal powerlessness in the face of her inability to stop or control her drinking.[1] "Lack of power, that was our dilemma."[2] We saw our need for a source of power outside of ourselves in order to have any hope of living each day without the necessity of drinking. Our entire recovery program started on this concept: "Our admissions of personal powerlessness finally turn out to be firm bedrock upon which happy and purposeful lives may be built."[3] From this point, we begin our recovery program seeking to find power outside of ourselves that can help us with our alcoholism.[4] We were quite certain that "no human power could have relieved our alcoholism,"[5] and so sought "a Power greater than ourselves."[6] And, happily, we found that "God could and would [help] if He were sought."[7] This initial contact with our Higher Power launches us into the deep work of recovery from our alcoholism.

Now, at the Eleventh Step, we find ourselves in need of power again. Obtaining some profound exposure to the knowledge of God's will for us, perhaps by more intuitive thinking or even direct inspiration, we now find ourselves in need of the power to actually carry that out. It is not enough to simply have the knowledge. Spiritual truth may actually be a danger to us unless it is brought into our lives and manifested. Often it is not the

---

[1] *Big Book,* at p. 24.
[2] *Big Book,* at p. 45.
[3] *Twelve and Twelve,* at p. 21.
[4] *Big Book,* at p. 45.

[5] *Big Book,* at p. 60.
[6] *Big Book,* at p. 45.
[7] *Big Book,* at p. 60.

knowledge that is difficult. Books can be read, seminars and retreats can be attended, practices can be studied. But the bringing of these things into actual practice in our lives is what connects us with the power behind the truth. And it is the connection with the power that propels us into our new sober lives in recovery. I think of this process of power as the moving of the knowledge of His will for me from my head to my heart. As more than one spiritual teacher has pointed out, the greatest distance any person travels is the movement from her head to her heart. It is at the level of my heart that the knowledge of His will for me will actually begin to influence my thoughts, speech, motives and acts. At the level of my head, it all remains abstract and theory. At the heart level, I will see actual change. The power is where my actions finally begin to become more consistent with my values.

Truths in general do not seem so difficult to me, though perhaps challenging. But a Truth in general that is confronting me and being made a Truth for me in particular is an altogether different matter. On the evening of September 11, 2001, I passed numerous signs outside of churches in my area announcing spontaneous prayer meetings for the victims and families of the terrorist attacks of the day in New York City, Washington, and Pennsylvania, and for the rescue workers. I attended two prayer vigils myself that evening. Living within commuting distance of New York City perhaps made the prayers even more impassioned. Subsequently, I attended a candlelight prayer vigil held outside in a field, continuing prayerful support for families and friends of the victims and the heroic efforts of the rescue workers. All this coming together as community in prayerful support of the victims of the terrorist attacks was wonderful compassionate practice. But I never saw a sign outside any church, nor did I ever find a prayer meeting to attend, that sought our prayers for the terrorist hijackers.

You have heard that it was said, 'You shall love your neighbor.' But I tell you, love your enemies, do good to those who hate you, bless those who curse you, and pray for those who mistreat you, so that you may be sons of your Father in heaven; for he makes his sun rise on the wicked and on the good, and sends rain to the righteous and to the unrighteous.

For if you love only those who love you, what credit is that to you: don't even the tax-gatherers do the same? And if you do good only to those who do good to you: don't even the Gentiles do the same? But love your enemies, and give, expecting nothing in return; and your reward will be great, and you will be sons of the Most High, for he is kind even to the ungrateful and the wicked. Therefore be merciful, just as your Father is merciful.[8]

After September 11th, this piece seems much more difficult than ever before. The Truth was always difficult, it's just that I did not really have to apply it. At the time Jesus spoke it, Palestine was an occupied country garrisoned with Roman soldiers and ruled by a Roman governor. The occupation was not pleasant. History records plenty of atrocities by the occupying government and soldiers. Yet, in the face of this "terror", Jesus spoke the above Truth. It was not an abstract Truth when he said it. It's not an abstract Truth to us now, either. But it's still a Truth, more so now than ever. To me, it was just a Truth in general prior to September 11th. Now it is a Truth in particular, and it challenges me to further spiritual growth.

It's not that prayers for victims, families, and friends of the terrorist attacks are the wrong thing to do. Certainly not. They are profoundly significant acts of compassion toward those suffering sudden and tragic grief. An act of compassion toward those suffering is always good and always right. But this is not the deep spiritual truth that Jesus taught. Praying for the victims and families is almost a natural response for most people confronted with tragedy at this level. Praying for the terrorist attackers is not; rather, it is a profoundly spiritual practice that challenges me to the core of my being. It is prayers for the terrorists themselves that will bring change to me at a deeply spiritual level. Prayer for those hurt will help the victims of the tragedy. But it is loving my enemies and praying for those who mistreat me that will make me a son of the Most High. Why?

---

[8]*The Bible,* Matthew 5:38-48.

The Spirituality of Sobriety

Because I then participate in the very nature of God as I have come to understand Him. This is how the God of my understanding acts. It is called unconditional love. And the knowledge of His will for us in regard to our enemies has been given to us for a couple thousand years. The power to carry it out is what I find lacking in my life. The knowledge is not the challenge. The power to act in accordance with the knowledge is the challenge. Knowledge is not where change occurs. Power is where change occurs.

Have we again moved too far from our program of recovery from alcoholism and the obsession to drink? I do not believe so. From the very beginning of my recovery, I have been confronted with this same challenge to take knowledge of spiritual truth and bring it into practice in my life. "The spiritual life is not a theory. *We have to live it.*"[9] Knowledge is not what saves us. At the First Step, we found that we were *"absolutely unable to stop drinking on the basis of self-knowledge."*[10] Having knowledge of our powerlessness over alcohol does not bring sobriety. It is when the power shows up in my life to make that truth real that I begin to recover.

If I have really grasped my utter powerlessness in the face of my obsession to drink, then my thinking and acting will change. I no longer engage in complicated plans and rituals to try to stop or control my drinking through various self-help methods. Rather, if I begin to act on the knowledge of my powerlessness, I will move into Second Step activity of seeking a Higher Power outside myself that can relieve my obsession and bring sanity. In other words, the knowledge of the powerlessness itself only leaves me stuck at the First Step – helpless and seemingly hopeless. The *Twelve and Twelve* introduces the Second Step with the exclamation of the one still trapped in the First Step, "Yes, you've got us over the barrel all right – but where do we go from here?"[11] When I begin to act like someone who has realized he does not have the power within himself to solve his problem, I begin looking for help outside myself. This is where I encounter

---

[9] *Big Book,* at p. 83.
[10] *Big Book,* at p. 39.
[11] *Twelve and Twelve,* at p. 25.

the power to act on the knowledge of my own powerlessness. And I then move to the next Step in my recovery program.

And so on through the entire Twelve Step recovery program. Studying about the development of the ego and the self-centered nature of human life is not the same as actually making the decision to turn my will and life over to the care of my Higher Power. I can do a thorough survey of successful inventories of recovering alcoholics, identifying the most important areas to cover, but this knowledge is nothing at all like actually taking pen in hand and writing down my own inventory of my conduct in regard to my primary instincts. Even this identifying of my own character defects remains only knowledge if I do not take the next Steps of actually asking my Higher Power to remove them from me. I could have advanced educational degrees in psychology, counseling and relationships, but this is not the same as actually compiling my list of people I have harmed and then making my amends to them. I could read all the latest self-help books on emotional intelligence, but that study is not the same as actually stopping myself in the midst of a negative emotional disturbance to take a Tenth Step spot-check inventory of my own ragged emotional state at that time. Again: "The spiritual life is not a theory. *We have to live it.*"[12] Sobriety does not come from knowledge. It comes from life transforming power bringing profound change within the alcoholic.

And so, now at the Eleventh Step, it remains the same. As we obtained knowledge of God's will for us in regard to our alcoholism and obsession to drink, we began to act in our lives as if this knowledge was true, and we found the power flowing into us to actually perform the work required of each of the Twelve Steps. It remains the same. As I move into my sober life, seeking to continue the practice of the principles in all my affairs, knowledge of God's will continues to confront me with choices for action as well as new values and beliefs. As I grow in this knowledge, I must continue to seek the power to bring it into manifestation in my life. I must act as if it

---

[12] *Big Book,* at p. 83.

The Spirituality of Sobriety

is true. Otherwise, I will again begin to find my thoughts, words and actions moving in a direction inconsistent with my new beliefs and values. And this inconsistency will once again create disturbance and pain within me that threaten my sobriety with occasions for drinking. The alcoholic simply has to live out his spirituality; it is a requirement for his continued long-term peaceful and contented sobriety.

Sometime back I gained some knowledge of a spiritual truth that I believe was knowledge of God's will for me in regard to relationships. The truth was simply that everything coming to me in relationship is only one of two things; it is always either a gift of love to me, or a request for love from me. Where I may perceive an attack, I can simply choose to see things differently, and I can then see the attack as actually a request for love.[13] I still believe this to be true. Now, for me, my prayer is for the power to carry this out in my life. To actually think, feel, speak and act in relationship as if the most blatant attack is simply the person's form of requesting love from me. To respond with love notwithstanding my own opinion of the person's inner or underlying motives. Today, when I act inconsistently with this spiritual truth, I find things showing up on my end-of-the-day Tenth Step inventory, and feel the need for periodic inventories on relationship issues to resolve the inconsistency in my beliefs and actions.

Knowledge, even knowledge of spiritual truth and God's will for me, is too easily used by my ego for its own purposes if it remains separate from my actual life experience. My ego does not care so much what game is played, as long as it remains in control of the playing. It can readily take on spiritual games as well as the pursuit of materialistic desires. As long as knowledge remains in my head, it is in the realm of my ego and available for its use in games. As soon as the knowledge moves from my head to my heart in the form of my prayer for the power to carry it out in my life, I encounter the humility found in my own inability to carry it out on my own resources. And this humility becomes the counter to my own ego's efforts to

---

[13] *A Course in Miracles* (Glen Ellen, CA: Foundation for Inner Peace, 1992).

162

run a game with the spiritual knowledge. It is the prayer for the power to carry out God's will in my life that brings the continued spiritual growth so necessary for my continuing contented sobriety. This is what checks egocentric efforts to co-opt the knowledge of God's will for me and restrict it to the limited realm of my abstract mind.

Reading the Twelve Steps from the poster on the wall at an A.A. meeting does not bring sobriety and recovery from alcoholism. We actually have to take them. Knowledge of the Steps just makes our drinking more painful. Connecting with the power to actually take them brings the recovery and sobriety. And so for the rest of our lives. Knowledge of God's will for us is only half of the story. I often hear people, in some desperation, talking of their need to know God's will for them in a particular circumstance, or of their prayers to obtain some direction from God about a particular matter. Today, I am grateful that the knowledge comes when it comes, and not necessarily when I demand it. Because I now know that the knowledge itself, without the power to carry it out in actual practice in my life, is not particularly helpful for me. I need, at the same time, both the knowledge and the power. If I presently lack the power, the knowledge may not be the best thing for me. But when the power comes, all things are possible. "As we felt new power flow in, as we enjoyed peace of mind, as we discovered we could face life successfully, as we became conscious of His presence, we began to lose our fear of today, tomorrow or the hereafter."[14]

---

[14] *Big Book,* at p. 63.

Chapter 16
Getting to Service

"Having had a spiritual awakening as the result of these
steps, we tried to carry this message to alcoholics …."

Step Twelve

The Twelfth Step! It was a long time and a lot of work getting here. But what awaits us here is the spiritual awakening discussed in the first chapters. In our new "awakened" state, we are now ready to take on Twelfth Step work doing two things we may never have done before in our lives. First, we are now prepared to be useful, to be of service to others. And, second, we are prepared to meet our God-given instinctual needs for sex, security and society, without causing hurt and turmoil to ourselves and others, by practicing the principles of the Steps in all our affairs. We can now take care of ourselves and our needs and, at the same time, help others less fortunate than us to meet their needs. What a change from the days of my drinking when I could hardly take care of myself and was continually demanding that others satisfy my needs!

My early recovery time had little to do with service to others. The focus was all on me and my new attempt at staying sober a day at a time. The theme of this phase of my recovery was: "Don't drink and go to meetings!" That was all I was trying to do. Certainly, it was all I was capable of doing. I did continue to hold a job during this period, though I can now see that discharge for drunkenness was just around the corner as I was doing some serious black-out drinking with customers while traveling overseas for my company. My wife threw me out of the house and my children stopped talking to me for quite some time. I was completely shut down and

The Spirituality of Sobriety

disconnected from all emotions. I went into psychological therapy to avoid a complete breakdown. As my sponsor told me repeatedly, "Gregg, the only thing you have to do today is not drink. None of the rest of it matters if you can't get through the day without drinking because you're going to lose it all anyway."

This period of my recovery was full of the negatives of recovery. I was physically detoxing on my own and drying out. The very concept of alcoholism as a disease was new to me. Seeing my powerlessness over my drinking was humiliating to me. The walls of denial that had protected my feeble sense of self-worth were cracking open and I was not happy with the kind of person I found behind the wall. I was dealing with the unmanageability of my life and the consequences of my late term drinking. Police and courts were part of my life as I worked my way through a DWI and a marital divorce early in recovery. I was attending A.A. meetings daily and desperately trying to understand why I drank the way I did and why I could never drink again.

But even while I was hard at work on the "Don't drink and go to meetings" phase of my recovery, I felt that there was more to this program than just drying out and cleaning up the consequences of my drinking. "Sometimes we hear an alcoholic say that the only thing he needs to do is to keep sober."[1] That was exactly what I had heard from my first week in recovery. Wasn't staying sober what we were supposed to be doing in recovery? "We feel a man is unthinking when he says that sobriety is enough."[2] So, if I do some thinking, I start to see that there is more involved in recovery than just not drinking and going to meetings. "Our liquor was but a symptom. So we had to get down to causes and conditions."[3] Just dealing with the alcohol and the drinking was not the complete plan of recovery. There was something underneath the drinking that was the cause.

---

[1] *Big Book*, at p. 82.
[2] *Big Book*, at p. 82.
[3] *Big Book*, at p. 64.

166

More sobriety brought about by the admission of alcoholism and by attendance at a few meetings is very good indeed, but it is bound to be a far cry from permanent sobriety and a contented, useful life. That is just where the remaining Steps of the A.A. program come in. Nothing short of continuous action upon these as a way of life can bring the much-desired result.[4]

And it would be the working of the rest of the Twelve Steps that would help me with the causes of my drinking and move me from the negatives of my early recovery to the positives of "a contented, useful life" in later recovery.

I now moved into the second phase of my recovery as I began working my way through the heart of the Steps: Three through Nine. I began to see my character defects, based on instincts run wild, as the primary cause of my drinking, and defective relationships as the immediate cause (Chapter 4 above). I began listing these things in my inventory and talking about them with my sponsor (Chapter 5). I tried to gain perspective on my debilitating selfishness and self-centeredness. The Third Step prayer became a daily part of my new morning devotional time (Chapter 8). I identified my more glaring resentments and worked hard at finding resolution through forgiveness (Chapter 7). I made my amends as best as I could at the time, primarily with my extended family (Chapter 10). Throughout all this, I was developing a prayer and meditation practice and seeking spiritual growth. Yet, through all this vital and necessary recovery work, and work I was convinced would need to continue for the rest of my life, I was also growing convinced, again, that there was something more to recovery than just this inside work on myself.

In the midst of discussing Steps Eight and Nine, the *Big Book* says: "At the moment we are trying to put our lives in order. But this is not an end in itself. Our real purpose is to fit ourselves to be of maximum service to God and the people about us."[5] And so I found myself moving into the third

---

[4] *Twelve and Twelve*, at pp. 39-40.
[5] *Big Book*, at p. 77.

phase of my recovery. I took on service obligations both within A.A. and in my community. While the work done in the heart of the Steps still continued, I found new capacity within myself to take on service work also. I was becoming useful!

Getting to service, the final phase of my recovery (?), is the expressly stated purpose of the Twelve Steps. The Forward to the *Twelve and Twelve* promises that if the alcoholic practices the Steps as a way of life, in addition to removing his drinking obsession, the Steps will "enable the sufferer to become happily and *usefully* whole."[6] Doctor Bob has listed several reasons why he took on service work, but the first one was simply from a sense of duty.[7] It's what we're supposed to be doing!

Service has actually been hard linked into my recovery from the beginning. I was just focused on other aspects, and missed the important pointers to service along the way. As I took on the Seventh Step prayer in my devotions in an effort to rid myself of character defects that I deeply regretted and desired with all my heart to have removed, I now see that my prayer was actually focused on requesting the removal of those defects that were blocking "my usefulness to [God] and to my fellows."[8] I do not know if all my defects fall into this category, but clearly the prayer is focused on cleaning me up for the purpose of getting me into service. Even the Third Step prayer, where I request God to take away my difficulties, is for the purpose of bearing witness of God's power and love to "those I would help."[9] For this prayer to be effective, it seems I need to be helping someone.

But we do not long continue in service from this sense of duty. The rewards of the practice of service are simply too great, and we soon find service work becoming our source of joy. As the early alcoholics continued in service, they found that the sense of duty, of service as a requirement in order to stay sober, became secondary. "It was transcended by the happiness they found in giving themselves for others."[10] Doctor Bob's

---

[6] *Twelve and Twelve*, at p. 15 (emphasis added).
[7] *Big Book*, at p. 181.
[8] *Big Book*, at p. 76.
[9] *Big Book*, at p. 63.
[10] *Big Book*, at p. 159.

second reason for taking on service work was because it was "a pleasure."[11] Even for the newcomer, there are "undreamed rewards" in the service work he is capable of doing.[12] While there is some recovery work to be done to prepare the newcomer for a life of service, there can be a vision even then of this work leading to "new mysteries, joys, and experiences of which he had never even dreamed."[13] Most all of us have had the experience of carrying the message to a suffering alcoholic, whether in the community, in rehab, or in A.A. meetings, and realizing that "no satisfaction has been deeper and no joy greater than in a Twelfth Step job well done."[14]

Service work engages us in the larger life around us. In helping others: "We think of their needs and work for them. This takes us out of ourselves."[15] As we are in service, we gain new perspective on ourselves and our own needs. We find that things we thought were so important are now less so because we have moved out of ourselves and become connected with a larger work in the world than the mere satisfaction of our old wants and desires.

The spirituality we develop in the course of our recovery is strongly linked to service work. Or, said the other way around, service work becomes an integral part of our new spirituality in recovery. First, we find that there is "nothing incompatible between a powerful spiritual experience and a life of sane and happy usefulness."[16] Then we find the further development of this spiritual experience requires service. For the recovering alcoholic, the way to "perfect and enlarge his spiritual life" is "through work and self-sacrifice for others."[17] Service work is what takes us beyond our old experiences and limited concepts of life to "new mysteries, joys and experiences."[18]

Finally, service work takes me full circle back to the sobriety I desperately sought in the first phase of my recovery. Working through the heart of the Steps in phase two of my recovery brought me relief from the

---

[11] *Big Book*, at p. 181.
[12] *Twelve and Twelve*, at p. 109.
[13] *Twelve and Twelve*, at p. 110.
[14] *Twelve and Twelve*, at p. 110.

[15] *Big Book*, at p. 70.
[16] *Big Book*, at p. 130.
[17] *Big Book*, at pp. 14-15.
[18] *Twelve and Twelve*, at p. 110.

obsession to drink.[19] But my service work in phase three is what builds "immunity from drinking" and provides "insurance" against a relapse. "Practical experience shows that nothing will so much insure immunity from drinking as intensive work with other alcoholics. It works when other activities fail."[20] This was Doctor Bob's last reason for taking on service work: "Because every time I do it I take out a little more insurance for myself against a possible slip."[21]

I worked my way through the wreckage and raw difficulties of my early recovery by not drinking and going to meetings. But there seemed to be more to recovery. Then I found release from the obsession to drink as I worked my way through the inside mess of my self-centeredness and character defects by moving through the heart of the Steps. But again, there seemed to be more to recovery. Then I found service work as my duty, my joy, and as an integral part of my spirituality. And finally, I found this service work to be the means by which I can gain confidence that I will never again have to go back to the painful work of the first phase of my recovery.

[19] *Twelve and Twelve*, at p. 15.
[20] *Big Book*, at p. 89.
[21] *Big Book*, at p. 181.

Chapter 17

Practicing the Principles in All Our Affairs (A Radical Change in Our Approach to the Instincts)

"Having had a spiritual awakening as the result of these steps, we tried ... to practice these principles in all our affairs."

Step Twelve

While service to others has become a major part of my recovery program and contributes significantly to my on-going sobriety today, I still have to find a way in sobriety to successfully meet my own instinctual needs for sex, security and society, as well as the basic troubles of life that continue to arise. The work here is to bring the practice of all Twelve Steps into every area of our daily lives. And the goal of this practice is that "we and those about us may find *emotional sobriety*."[1] There is great

---
[1] *Twelve and Twelve*, at p. 106 (emphasis added).

significance to the use of the term "emotional sobriety" here. Remember, the goal in Step Ten was emotional balance. Now we are looking for something a bit different. The definition of sober that I like in connection with my emotions at this Step is: "Devoid of frivolity, excess, exaggeration, or speculative imagination; straightforward.... Marked by circumspection and self-restraint."[2] This is how I envision the result of the practice of the principles in all my affairs. My emotions are serious to me, not frivolous, and they are not excessive, exaggerated or made up. They are quite straightforward. My approach to my emotions is circumspect, and I continue to exercise the self-restraint I developed in my Tenth Step.

The chapter on the Twelfth Step in the *Twelve and Twelve* is by far the longest chapter in the book. At the Step meetings I have attended we divide the text and cover the material over two or three meetings. I have found the following outline of the chapter to be useful in my readings. We are first introduced to the Twelfth Step, and then given a discussion of the spiritual awakening beginning at page 106. Then at page 109, we are asked, "Now, what about the rest of the Twelfth Step?" Here begins the discussion of carrying the message. At page 111, we are asked, "What about the practice of these principles in *all* our affairs?" And now for the rest of chapter, we are introduced to this new practice, and given the tools for a radical new approach to the living of our lives. This section of the chapter discussing the practice of the principles in all our affairs, from pages 111 to 125, is longer than any whole chapter covering any other Step in the *Twelve and Twelve*. More text is devoted to this new practice than to the discussion of any other Step. This should give us some understanding of its importance to our ongoing recovery, as well as the work involved in the practice.

This last part of the Twelfth Step presents to us "the biggest question yet."[3] Can we do it? Can we take the practice of the principles we used in relation to our drinking and now take them into every area of our lives? Can we apply them to all our troubles and every problem of our lives just like

---

[2] *The American Heritage Dictionary of the English Language*, 4th edition.
[3] *Twelve and Twelve*, at p. 111.

we did to our alcoholism? The goal is to take into our family lives and daily work the same spirit of "love and tolerance" and "confidence and faith" that we found in A.A.; to meet our responsibilities in the world as we do in A.A.; and to bring devotion to the religion of our choice as we do to our A.A. meetings.[4] It is time to move out from our isolated and protected shelter we find in A.A. and become engaged in life again, but on a wholly new and radical basis as discussed in the remaining pages of the *Twelve and Twelve.* There are at least two reasons for insisting on this new approach to living. First, to assure against a relapse most certain to occur if we went back to our old ways and patterns of living. Second, and on a more positive note, to "improve our chances for really happy and useful living."[5] We are not to remain isolated in our recovery. "While you were drinking, you were withdrawing from life little by little. Now you are getting back into the social life of this world."[6] And the last section of the Twelfth Step makes this possible.

The new practice of the principles in all our affairs is introduced to us in the context of meeting our troubles in life. We are not speaking of the troubles that arose from our destructive alcoholism, those troubles that were "basically of our own making" first addressed in our Fourth Step.[7] Rather, here we are speaking of our "basic troubles" that are "the same as everyone else's."[8] Remember, by this time we have done what we could do about those troubles of our own making from our drinking past. Now we are looking forward to our new life, and getting educated about how to deal soberly with the "basic troubles" of life which everyone encounters.

The *Twelve and Twelve* divides our basic troubles into two groups. First, the text discusses the "great big lump that we can't begin to swallow."[9] These are the tragic events of life that totally redirect our course: job loss, divorce or separation, bereavement and loss of loved ones. Note, if these tragic events are coming to us as a consequence of our drinking, then they are Fourth Step matters. However, if they are coming to us in our

---

[4] *Twelve and Twelve*, at pp. 111-12.
[5] *Twelve and Twelve*, at p. 114.
[6] *Big Book*, at p. 102.

[7] *Big Book*, at p. 62.
[8] *Twelve and Twelve*, at p. 114.
[9] *Twelve and Twelve*, at p. 113.

The Spirituality of Sobriety

sobriety, then they are Twelfth Step matters. For example, if I lost my job because I got fired for drinking during working hours, then I need to deal with this issue in the context of the Fourth Step. However, if I lost my job because of a general reduction-in-force type layoff, notwithstanding my outstanding job performance, then I have a Twelfth Step issue. The Twelfth Step practice is to make it through the tragedy by bravely meeting the calamity with faith, turning the loss to an asset, all the while remaining a comfort to myself and others. How do I do all that? By the help and grace of God that flows into us as we continue to practice the principles in all our affairs right through the tragedy. The help and grace of God is expressly mentioned three times in this short piece on meeting the "big lumps" in our lives successfully.[10]

The second group of troubles are "the lesser and more continuous problems of life."[11] These are the problems that show up everyday in our lives, some on a repeating basis. Some of my personal favorites: stuck in traffic, long lines, picking the line or lane that then doesn't move, broken appliances, flat tires, medical conditions, unanticipated budget-breaking expenses, three days of rain at the start of a backpacking trip, etc. The Twelfth Step's answer to these problems of life? More spiritual development! The text comes back to this solution to our problems of life repeatedly:

"Our answer is in still more **spiritual development**,"[12]

"And as we **grow spiritually**...,"[13]

"But when we are willing to place **spiritual growth** first,"[14]

"After we come into A.A., if we go on **growing**...,"[15]

"As we made **spiritual progress**...,"[16]

"When we **developed still more**...,"[17]

---

[10] *Twelve and Twelve*, at pp. 113-14.
[11] *Twelve and Twelve*, at p. 114.
[12] *Twelve and Twelve*, at p. 114.
[13] *Twelve and Twelve*, at p. 114.
[14] *Twelve and Twelve*, at p. 114.
[15] *Twelve and Twelve*, at p. 115.
[16] *Twelve and Twelve*, at p. 115.
[17] *Twelve and Twelve*, at p. 116.

Practicing the Principles in all our Affairs

"… but it did matter what our **spiritual condition** was,"[18]

Speaking of the recent break-up of her romantic relationship, a tearful woman with several years of good sobriety quite poignantly said in an A.A. meeting I attended, "I know, I know, don't tell me; it's just an opportunity for more f_____ spiritual development!" It *is* the Twelfth Step's answer to our problems in life.

But there is a specific form this Twelfth Step spiritual growth takes. This is not about more religious devotion, or taking on more spiritual practices from a tradition. Prayer and meditation, remember, are our Eleventh Step practice; these are the means by which we improve our conscious contact with God as we understand Him. In the Twelfth Step we are presented with a spiritual development that will enable us to meet our life problems head on and do well in the process. The form of spirituality and practice presented throughout our literature is nothing celestial or spooky. It is not about God showing up in our lives and mysteriously solving all our problems for us. It is not about increased faith or being transformed into spiritual beings who have no problems here on earth. All these things would certainly be wonderful experiences, but they simply are not the direction of the spiritual growth in our Twelfth Step practice of the principles in all our affairs. We should also note that the Twelfth Step answer to our life problems is not the solution often gratuitously offered up in the course of an A.A. meeting: "Keep comin' back!" and "Don't drink and go to meetings!" While this is great advice, the Twelfth Step offers a different answer. The Twelfth Step does not belittle either the problems of life or the solution to them. "For it is only by accepting and solving our problems that we can begin to get right with ourselves and with the world about us, and with Him who presides over us all."[19]

The Twelfth Step answer to our problems is much more practical, cutting right to the heart of matters, right to the causes of our alcoholism:

---

[18] *Twelve and Twelve*, at p. 122.
[19] *Twelve and Twelve*, at p. 125.

The Spirituality of Sobriety

"And as we grow spiritually, we find that our old attitudes toward our instincts need to undergo *drastic revisions*."[20] This theme of "drastic revision" is reiterated in relation to each instinctual need as they are subsequently discussed one after another:

> **Security** – "After we come into A.A., if we go on growing, our attitudes and actions toward security – emotional security and financial security – commence to *change profoundly*."[21]

> **Financial Security** – "Where the possession of money and material things was concerned, our outlook underwent the same *revolutionary change*."[22]

> **Sex and Family Relations** – "He *persistently tries* all of A.A.'s Twelve Steps in his home, often with fine results."[23]

> **Society** – "Let's here take note of our *improved outlook* upon the problems of personal importance, power, ambition, and leadership."[24]

The spiritual growth that the Twelfth Step invites is a radical change in our approach to the instincts. And it is here that we find the true meaning of practicing the principles in all our affairs:

> Our desires for emotional security and wealth, for personal prestige and power, for romance, and for family satisfactions – all these have to be tempered and redirected. We have learned that the satisfaction of instincts cannot be the sole end and aim of our lives. If we place instincts first, we have got the cart before the horse; we shall be pulled backward into disillusionment. But when we are willing to place spiritual growth first – then and only then do we have a real chance.[25]

---

[20] *Twelve and Twelve*, at p. 114 (emphasis added).

[21] *Twelve and Twelve*, at p. 115 (emphasis added).

[22] *Twelve and Twelve*, at p. 120 (emphasis added).

[23] *Twelve and Twelve*, at p. 119 (emphasis added).

[24] *Twelve and Twelve*, at p. 122 (emphasis added).

[25] *Twelve and Twelve*, at p. 114.

Practicing the Principles in all our Affairs

Here, again, are those instincts for sex, security and society we first met back in our Fourth Step work (Chapters 5 and 6 above). Those God-given instinctual needs that every human being pursues for his good; those instincts that alcoholics pursue past their normal bounds, permitting them to drive our thinking and behavior, until they become our character defects. And so, here at the Twelfth Step, we take on a radically new practice in relation to our instinctual needs for sex, security and society. The desire itself is "tempered and redirected" from its old pattern and course. "We have learned that the satisfaction of instincts cannot be the sole end and aim of our lives."[26] Where did we learn this lesson? In the course of working our way through the Steps in our recovery. If we allow the instinctual needs to become "the sole end and aim or our lives," then that becomes "the measure of our character defects."[27] The way we prevent our instinctual needs from becoming new character defects, as we go forward in our new sober life, is by placing spiritual growth first – as more important than the satisfaction of instincts – and so continue the practice of the principles in all our affairs.

Why does this new practice in regard to our instincts work for the alcoholic? Because it goes right to the underlying causes of our alcoholism we have already identified in Chapter 4. Our character defects, "representing instincts gone astray," have been "the primary cause" of our drinking, and our "defective relations with other human beings" have been "the immediate cause" of our alcoholism.[28] This radical new approach to our instincts presented in the Twelfth Step prevents character defects from arising from our instinctual needs. And, as we learn to properly obtain the satisfaction of our instinctual needs, we find our relationships with others changing from defective to effective, functional and pleasing. So, the primary and immediate causes of our drinking, that we dealt with so much in the course of our recovery work through the Steps, do not re-appear as

---

[26] *Twelve and Twelve*, at p. 114.
[27] *Twelve and Twelve*, at p. 65.
[28] *Twelve and Twelve*, at pp. 50 and 80.

we go forward in our new sober lives. This last part of the Twelfth Step is A.A.'s relapse prevention program.

The rest of the *Twelve and Twelve* chapter on the Twelfth Step now focuses, one after another, on each of the instinctual needs, discussing the radical change in our approach to each one. The discussion of the instinctual need for emotional security begins on page 115. We turn to the instinct for sex and family relations on page 117. Then we return to financial security on page 120. Finally, the instinctual need for society is discussed from page 122 to the end of the chapter. Before beginning here, we might pause to remember that the recovering alcoholic has already made "a rough survey of his conduct with respect to his primary instincts for sex, security, and society" in his Fourth Step inventory.[29] This survey revealed our character defects. As we take on the practice of the principles in all our affairs, we will begin to find "drastic revisions" and "revolutionary change" in our new conduct in sobriety toward these same instinctual needs. As we progress in our Twelfth Step practice, we will find profound changes occurring in our new lives when compared to the dysfunctional lives outlined in our Fourth Step inventories.

Emotional Security. Our unreasonable demand for this instinctual need beyond its normal bounds had created "unworkable relations with other people" where we "had tried to play God and dominate those about us, or we had insisted on being overdependent upon them."[30] Either way, the relationship was unworkable, and we ended up either "bitterly hurt" because people resisted us, or disillusioned because they let us down. The radical change in our pursuit of the need for emotional security results in a "partnership or brotherhood with all those around us."[31] We stopped trying to be either on top or on the bottom, and instead assumed a side-by-side position with others. We then placed our dependence upon God and so "discovered the best possible source of emotional stability."[32] With these

---

[29] *Twelve and Twelve,* at p. 50.
[30] *Twelve and Twelve*, at p. 115.

[31] *Twelve and Twelve*, at p. 116.
[32] *Twelve and Twelve*, at p. 116.

Practicing the Principles in all our Affairs

"new attitudes," we find that we are not so "deeply shaken by the shortcomings of others or by any calamity not of our own making."[33] **Sex and Family Relations**. Three separate types of situations are presented here for discussion: the marriage wracked by previous alcoholic drinking, the new marriage made in sobriety, and the single person. For the alcoholic marriage, the radical change here is to stop insisting on things being done our way, even in recovery, and become aware of the damage we have inflicted on mates and children. "When the distortion has been great, however, a long period of patient striving may be necessary."[34] Under the new approach, the alcoholic "takes up his marriage responsibilities with a willingness," and "persistently tries all of A.A.'s Twelve Steps in his home."[35] For the new marriage in sobriety, the radical change is to seek "compatibility at spiritual, mental, and emotional levels," and to make sure there is "no deep-lying emotional handicap in either."[36] For the single person, the radical change is finding his "partnership with others" and becoming involved in projects and enterprises unavailable to the person with marital and family responsibilities. "We daily see such members render prodigies of service, and receive great joys in return."[37]

Financial Security. Our old pattern in regard to financial security was to play the spendthrift, impressing people with our spending, or to play the miser hoarding money to finance the next binge or, in sobriety, to replenish losses accumulated in our drinking. The radical change in regard to this instinctual need was to stop the absolute insistence upon financial security at any cost, and move from faith in ourselves to provide our material needs to faith in God to provide for us. "It did not matter much what our material condition was, but it did matter what our spiritual condition was. Money gradually became our servant and not our master. It became a means of exchanging love and service with those about us."[38]

---

[33] *Twelve and Twelve*, at p. 116.
[34] *Twelve and Twelve*, at p. 118.
[35] *Twelve and Twelve*, at p. 119.

[36] *Twelve and Twelve*, at p. 119.
[37] *Twelve and Twelve*, at p. 120.
[38] *Twelve and Twelve*, at p. 122.

Society. Our old pattern was one of grandiosity. "We simply had to be number one people to cover up our deep-lying inferiorities."[39] The radical change in our approach to this instinctual need is to "no longer strive to dominate or rule those about us in order to gain self-importance."[40] We found that "we do not have to be specially distinguished among our fellows in order to be useful and profoundly happy."[41] And these "permanent and legitimate satisfactions of right living" we found to be sufficient.[42]

So what is the guidance I receive from the Twelfth Step in relation to my instinctual needs and the problems of life I will certainly encounter as I go forward in my new sobriety? Well, by now I have become convinced that I have "more problems than alcohol," and that these problems make me unhappy and may threaten my sobriety.[43] I have been assured that my "many troubles, now made more acute because [I] cannot use alcohol to kill the pain, can be solved, too."[44] And I do believe that "spiritual principles would solve all my problems," not just my alcoholism.[45] So how does this happen? What am I supposed to do? It's like the Sufi mystic on retreat who, in the silence and solitude of a lone hut in the woods, was desperately seeking a solution to a particular problem in his life:

> In this state I knew the answer to my life's dilemma was available.
> I asked my soul for its guidance, and understood the answer
> through all the subtle layers of my ego. When I asked what I was
> to do, the answer was clear: *Just keep doing what you are
> already doing.*[46]

We worked our way through all Twelve Steps in the course of our recovery from alcoholism. Now that we "have recovered," and "have solved the drink problem,"[47] what do we do about life's problems? We keep doing what we are already doing! We keep practicing those principles in all our affairs!

---

[39] *Twelve and Twelve*, at p. 123.
[40] *Twelve and Twelve*, at p. 124.
[41] *Twelve and Twelve*, at p. 124.
[42] *Twelve and Twelve*, at p. 124.
[43] *Twelve and Twelve*, at p. 39.
[44] *Twelve and Twelve*, at p. 39.
[45] *Big Book*, at p. 42.
[46] *That Which Transpires Behind That Which Appears*, at. p. x.
[47] *Big Book*, at p. 17.

Chapter 18
So Why Does It Take a Spiritual Awakening?

*"We know that a spiritual experience is the key
to survival from alcoholism and that for most of
us it is the only key. We must awake or die."*

Language of the Heart

For years, I read the Twelfth Step as containing three separate parts. This approach was reinforced by my home group Step Meeting where we took three weeks to cover the Twelfth Step, one part a week. First we discussed the spiritual awakening,[1] then the carrying of the message,[2] and finally the practice of the principles in all our affairs.[3] However, today I read the Twelfth Step as only two parts: carrying the message and the practice of the principles. The first part concerning the spiritual awakening is a statement of the condition in which I undertake these two activities. The grammar seems to me to require this reading. It's not that I undertake service work, it's that I undertake service work after having had a spiritual awakening. What makes service work and the continued practice of the principles part of a Twelfth Step practice is the doing of these things in the context of a spiritual awakening. It's about an attitude toward the work and the underlying reason why I am undertaking the work.

---

[1] *Twelve and Twelve*, at pp. 106-109.
[2] *Twelve and Twelve*, at pp. 109-111.
[3] *Twelve and Twelve*, at pp. 111-125.

The Spirituality of Sobriety

Why is a spiritual awakening a pre-requisite to carrying the message to other alcoholics and practicing the principles in all my affairs? In working with another alcoholic, I am advised to "Tell him exactly what happened to you. Stress the spiritual feature freely.... The main thing is that he is willing to believe in a Power greater than himself and that he live by spiritual principles."[4] If I have yet to have a spiritual awakening myself, it will be difficult for me to speak of "the spiritual feature" convincingly from my own experience. "But obviously you cannot transmit something you haven't got. See to it that your relationship with Him is right, and great events will come to pass for you and countless others."[5] And, more practically, if I show up with a condescending attitude that the alcoholic needs my help, I will be totally ineffectual. If I have awakened, then I show up as part of my own recovery program, giving away for free what I myself have received from others for free, and I may or may not find myself being of some usefulness to the alcoholic. As one old-timer says: "I've been on hundreds of Twelfth Step calls, and they were all successful. I've stayed sober!"

As to the continued practice of the Steps in my life, I have found the spiritual awakening to be essential. In sobriety, I still find myself working on issues of self-centeredness, relationship difficulties and character defects through the Steps. And now I can no longer "blame" these things on the effects of my drinking. No, I am doing these things while cold stone sober. The spiritual awakening has opened me up to this deeper, higher part of myself that I now begin to relate to more. I can more easily and less painfully acknowledge the character defects and give them up, instead of feeling that they are an integral part of me and finding myself justifying and defending them to the bitter end in an effort to protect "myself." I find great comfort in this spiritual awakening as I continue to bring into conscious awareness aspects of myself that I had long hidden away in denial and rationalization.

---

[4] *Big Book*, at p. 93.
[5] *Big Book,* at p. 164.

So Why Does It Take a Spiritual Awakening?

But, from the beginning, I have wondered about this question at even a more basic level: Why is a spiritual awakening part of my program of recovery from alcoholism? Our literature is pretty clear that if I am an alcoholic who has lost his ability to control his drinking, then only a spiritual experience will bring recovery.[6] "To begin with, a spiritual awakening is our means of finding sobriety. To us of A.A. sobriety means life itself. We know that a spiritual experience is the key to survival from alcoholism and that for most of us it is the only key. We must awake or die."[7] Having gotten sober, I do not remain sober if I do not continue in my spiritual awakening: "We are not cured of alcoholism. What we really have is a daily reprieve contingent on the maintenance of our spiritual condition."[8]

As I made progress in the program working my way through the early Steps, I began to see the hopelessness of my condition and that I would need help from something bigger than me if I was to beat alcohol's grip on my mind and body. I could readily see that lack of power was my problem,[9] and that I tapped into "new power" when I was "conscious of His presence."[10] And it worked! I got sober. I felt like one of those who "have recovered" and "solved the drink problem."[11] Since "the problem has been removed,"[12] my question became: Why can't I just go back to getting busy again in my own life? Why all this continued insistence on a spiritual awakening? As one fellow put it:

> But now that I've gone ex-grog, what's the matter with trying to live my old life? That was okay, until the liquor got me. I was going places, on the way to making my pile. Things weren't too bad at home, either, until my wife yelled she'd had enough of me, and left. All I need is sobriety, and A.A. can keep on giving me that. Now I can go about my business. I'm sure I can make a better job of it this time.[13]

---

[6] *Big Book*, at p. 44.
[7] *The Language of the Heart*, at pp. 233-34.
[8] *Big Book*, at p. 85.
[9] *Big Book* at p. 45.

[10] *Big Book*, at p. 63.
[11] *Big Book*, at p. 17.
[12] *Big Book*, at p. 85.
[13] *The Language of the Heart*, at p. 234.

The Spirituality of Sobriety

The assumption here is that we were in pretty good shape before our drinking took off. "This being so, we think it logically follows that sobriety – first, last, and all the time – is the only thing we need to work for. We believe that our one-time good characters will be revived the moment we quit alcohol."[14]

The answer for me did not come directly. This was the point where it was very important for me to just keep doing the recovery work. The literature tells us that "the change in our attitude toward God" does not happen until we begin gaining humility in the course of our Seventh Step work.[15] What is this change in attitude?

> We began to get over the idea that the Higher Power was a sort of bush-league pinch hitter, to be called upon only in an emergency. The notion that we would still live our own lives, God helping a little now and then, began to evaporate. Many of us who had thought ourselves religious awoke to the limitations of this attitude. Refusing to place God first, we had deprived ourselves of His help. But now the words "Of myself I am nothing, the Father doeth the works" began to carry bright promise and meaning.[16]

With a bit more humility, the answer did come. I would need that new-found power on a continuing basis. Just as I found the spiritual awakening helpful to me in the process of swallowing and digesting those "big chunks of truth" about myself in my Fourth Step,[17] I could now see the need for the awakening to allow me to stay in this new truth. And I found it to be necessary for slowing down the onslaught of my character defects. Fear is the "chief activator of our defects,"[18] and I have found the "basic antidote for fear is a spiritual awakening."[19] This recovery from alcoholism was not a one-time job. I will need help on a daily basis in order to keep growing in recovery and moving away from that next drink. As one of Rumi's poems says:

---

[14] *Twelve and Twelve*, at p. 45.
[15] *Twelve and Twelve*, at p. 75.
[16] *Twelve and Twelve*, at p. 75.

[17] *Big Book*, at p. 71.
[18] *Twelve and Twelve*, at p. 76.
[19] *The Best of Bill*, at p. 17.

184

So Why Does It Take a Spiritual Awakening?

Pale sunlight
pale the wall.

Love moves away.
The light changes.

I need more grace
than I thought.[20]

"We are not cured of alcoholism. What we really have is a daily reprieve contingent on the maintenance of our spiritual condition."[21]

I need the spiritual awakening as my relapse prevention program, and as the means for realizing "the theme of A.A.'s Twelfth Step:" the joy of living.[22] In the course of working my way through the Steps as the means of relieving the obsession to drink in early sobriety, I repeatedly found myself interrupting my normal life activities to seemingly step outside of my life in order to undertake the work. I sat by myself quietly at home preparing my Fourth Step inventory. In solitary prayer, I turned my life over to my Higher Power and humbly asked Him to remove my character defects. I took time from my normal schedule to visit my sponsor and make my Fifth Step admissions. I stopped a typical daily interchange in a relationship with a loved one in order to sit down and open my past conduct, making my amends as best as I could. And I interrupt an emotional disturbance right as it is happening to take my Tenth Step spot-check inventory. In other words, I stepped outside of life in order to take on the recovery work of the Steps. As a result of this work in the Steps, I achieved a spiritual awakening at the Twelfth Step. But this awakening occurred *outside of life*. Now, the goal, as I take on the Twelfth Step practice of the principles in all my affairs, is to *awaken in life*.

---

[20] *The Essential Rumi*, at p. 53.
[21] *Big Book*, at p. 85.
[22] *Twelve and Twelve,* at pp. 106 and 125.

185

The Spirituality of Sobriety

This distinction of awakening outside of life and awakening in life parallels practices from other spiritual traditions. In the Sufi practice, for instance, it is taught:

> awakening beyond life must occur before we can awaken in life.... What this means is that one sometimes has to call a halt to daily life, either through a disciplined regimen of daily meditations or, if possible, by going on a retreat. It's as if we must take a break from the demands of everyday life in order to awaken a part of ourselves that has been asleep. Then, when we return to life, the task is to remain awake.[23]

The challenge for me in the Twelfth Step is to enter a conference room for a business meeting where a lot of heavy-duty egos are attempting to blame others and justify themselves, and take my seat at the table and awaken. To come up on the worst interstate traffic jam in history, and bring the car to a stop and awaken. To choose the line at the grocery store that stops moving, and hold my groceries and awaken. To realize that I have said something less than compassionate, and sit down with my lover and awaken. To have an abused teenager with behavior problems I have been working with suggest that I should "eat sh_t and die," and stand before him and awaken. To take the spiritual awakening I encountered outside of life in my recovery work, and now bring that awakening right into the midst of my life. To awaken in life! To interrupt my normal reactions, my patterns of behavior as detailed in my Fourth Step inventory, and to respond differently. To awaken right as the words are being said, the actions are being taken. To take my part in the conversation, to move appropriately in the scene, but in an awakened state. To practice the principles in *all* my affairs.

The alternative is to go back to living my life by my old ways, get beat up over time, step out of my life and drag myself back to an A.A. meeting grateful to have made it in the door still sober, get my dose of awakening,

---

[23] Pir Vilayat Inayat Khan, *Awakening: A Sufi Experience* (New York: Jeremy P. Tarcher/ Putnam, 1999), at pp. 43-44.

So Why Does It Take a Spiritual Awakening?

and then go back to my life. I can attend an A.A. meeting every day and continue this painful practice for a long time. Or, I can choose to awaken in life, move through the day's activities in a more awakened state, and then attend my A.A. meeting in the abundance of life's blessings from the day, contributing happily when it is my time to share at the meeting. I am much less relapse prone. And, in this lighter, more awakened state, I finally begin to experience that "joy of good living" the Twelfth Step so affirmatively states as its theme.

The spiritual awakening is also required because the problem we deal with is, at its core, spiritual. In A.A. meetings, we often hear as part of the alcoholic's story that she felt awkward, disconnected and out-of-place with people and the world around her. She felt there was something fundamentally wrong with her from an early age even before the onset of alcoholic drinking. As one fellow in our A.A. meetings likes to say, "I felt like I got dropped off by a space ship and left on my own." The solution to this fundamental life problem is spiritual. William James concluded that all religious experience is based on two things: an uneasiness and its solution.

1. The uneasiness, reduced to its simplest terms, is a sense that there is *something wrong about us* as we naturally stand.
2. The solution is a sense that *we are saved from the wrongness* by making proper connection with the higher powers.[24]

This is the fundamental problem we face as an alcoholic: There is something wrong with us that only a Higher Power can solve. William James provides a description of the spiritual experiences that bring the solution:

> They allow for the divided self and the struggle; they involve the change of personal center and the surrender of the lower self; they express the appearance of exteriority of the helping power and yet account for our sense of union with it; and they fully justify our feelings of security and joy.[25]

---

[24] *The Varieties of Religious Experience,* at p. 383.
[25] *The Varieties of Religious Experience,* at p. 384.

187

The Spirituality of Sobriety

This is the description of the work on "the root of our troubles," the self-centeredness that I first encountered in the Third Step, and whose manifestations I have dealt with during my work on the Fourth through Ninth Steps.

Many spiritual traditions speak of this work. In mystical Christianity, it is Paul's revelation that "I live; yet not I, but Christ liveth in me; and the life which I now live in the flesh I live by the faith of the Son of God."[26] In Sufism, we speak of *fana* – the need to "die before you die." This dying to self *is* the awakening! Religion is about saving the soul; spirituality is about losing it. Religion talks of the soul in paradise in heaven. Spirituality talks of losing the soul and only God knowing Himself. Total union into the eternal – no longer subject/object. No duality. The knower, known and the knowing are all one thing. The lover, the beloved, and the loving exist together as one.

A certain person came to the Friend's door
and knocked.
                    "Who's there?"
"It's me."

The Friend answered, "Go away. There's no place
for raw meat at this table."

The individual went wandering for a year.
Nothing but the fire of separation
can change hypocrisy and ego. The person returned
completely cooked,
walked up and down in front of the Friend's house,
gently knocked.
                    "Who is it?"
"You."

---

[26] *The Bible,* Galatians 2:20.

188

So Why Does It Take a Spiritual Awakening?

"Please come in, my self,
there's no place in this house for two.
The doubled end of the thread is not what goes through
the eye of the needle.
It's a single-pointed, fined-down, thread end,
not a big ego-beast with baggage."

But how can a camel be thinned to a thread?
With the shears of practices, with *doing* things.

And with the help from the one who brings
impossibilities to pass, who quiets willfulness,
who gives sight to one blind from birth.

. . . .

Every holy person seems to have a different doctrine
and practice, but there's really only one work.[27]

We die to the self-centeredness – the very root of our trouble. And we find our freedom from the compulsion to drink. If this "dying to self" seems too extreme as a concept for simple recovery from alcoholism, if it seems we have gone much too far into some mystical experience, we might be reminded that we said: "Above everything, we alcoholics must be rid of this selfishness.... And there often seems no way of *entirely getting rid of self* without His aid."[28] From the beginning of our recovery program, our Third Step prayer has been: "God, ... Relieve me of the bondage of self." Because this self-centeredness is the root of our troubles, the work of the Steps is focused on "entirely getting rid of the self."[29] As we have found, all the Steps "deflate our ego."[30] I have found the A.A. recovery program's insistence on this "entirely getting rid of self" to be quite consistent with the work of other spiritual traditions leading to an awakening.

---

[27] *The Essential Rumi,* at pp. 87-88.
[28] *Big Book*, at p. 62 (emphasis added).
[29] *Big Book*, at p. 62.

[30] *Twelve and Twelve,* at p. 55.

The Spirituality of Sobriety

Why does it take a spiritual awakening to come out of the self-centeredness? Simply because I cannot do this work myself. "Neither could we reduce our self-centeredness much by wishing or trying on our own power. We had to have God's help."[31] And there is no way to effectively move out of the self-centeredness other than by turning our will and lives over to something else. There is nothing else other than the spiritual plane that effectively works as the recipient of our will and lives. If we turn everything over to a spouse, we end up with a co-dependent relationship at best. If we turn it over to our children, we will most probably take on a martyr or victim role over time. If we turn it over to others in service, we are likely to eventually experience burn out. If we turn it over to a religious movement, we become cult-like. If we turn it over to a political or social cause, we are sure to become disillusioned at some point. The only place to go with our will and lives is to God, or our spiritually-based Higher Power; there is simply no other effective way out of the self-centeredness.

And so, we find it all comes down to this self-centeredness. We should not be surprised since we identified this as the root of the trouble long ago. "Above everything, we alcoholics must be rid of this selfishness. We must, or it kills us!"[32] It is more important than anything else in the recovery program. And we have seen the Third Step theme repeating itself throughout the course of our work on the Steps. In fact, we found that the "other Steps of the A.A. program can be practiced with success only when Step Three is given a determined and persistent trial."[33] And, we may remember that we said: "the effectiveness of the whole A.A. program will rest upon how well and earnestly we have tried to come to 'a decision to turn our will and our lives over to the care of God *as we understood Him*.*"[34] The *Big Book* concludes its text portion with the suggestion: "Abandon yourself to God as you understand God...."[35] I can think of no more fitting way to conclude a study on the spirituality of sobriety than by repeating our Third Step Prayer:

[31] *Big Book,* at p. 62.
[32] *Big Book*, at p. 62.
[33] *Twelve and Twelve*, at p. 40.

[34] *Twelve and Twelve*, at pp. 34-35.
[35] *Big Book,* at p. 164.

So Why Does It Take a Spiritual Awakening?

God, I offer myself to Thee – to build with me and to do with me as Thou wilt. Relieve me of the bondage of self, that I may better do Thy will. Take away my difficulties, that victory over them may bear witness to those I would help of Thy Power, Thy Love, and Thy Way of life. May I do Thy will always!

Amen.

Twelve Steps of Alcoholics Anonymous

1. Admitted we were powerless over alcohol – that our lives had become unmanageable.

2. Came to believe that a Power greater than ourselves could restore us to sanity.

3. Made a decision to turn our will and our lives over to the care of God *as we understood Him.*

4. Made a searching and fearless moral inventory of ourselves.

5. Admitted to God, to ourselves, and to another human being the exact nature of our wrongs.

6. Were entirely ready to have God remove all these defects of character.

7. Humbly asked Him to remove our shortcomings.

8. Made a list of all persons we had harmed, and became willing to make amends to them all.

9. Made direct amends to such people wherever possible, except when to do so would injure them or others.

10. Continued to take personal inventory and when we were wrong promptly admitted it.

11. Sought through prayer and meditation to improve our conscious contact with God *as we understood Him*, praying only for knowledge of His will for us and the power to carry that out.

12. Having had a spiritual awakening as the result of these steps, we tried to carry this message to alcoholics, and to practice these principles in all our affairs.

Prayers in Recovery

Third Step Prayer

God, I offer myself to you – to build with me and to do with me as you will.

Relieve me of the bondage of self, that I may better do thy will.

Take away my difficulties, that victory over them may bear witness to those I would help of thy power, thy love, and thy way of life.

May I do thy will always. Amen.

Seventh Step Prayer

God, I am now willing that you should have all of me, good and bad.

I pray that you now remove from me every single defect of character which stands in the way of my usefulness to you and my fellows.

Grant me strength, as I go out from here, to do your bidding. Amen.

Eleventh Step Prayer
(Saint Francis Prayer)

Lord, make me an instrument of your peace.

Where there is hatred, let me sow love;
Where there is injury, pardon and a spirit of forgiveness;
Where there is discord, union;
Where there is doubt, faith;
Where there is despair, hope;

Where there is darkness, light;
Where there is sadness, joy.

Grant that I may not so much seek to be consoled as to console;
To be understood as to understand;
To be loved as to love.
For it is in giving that we receive;
It is in pardoning that we are pardoned;
And it is in dying that we are born to eternal life.

Serenity Prayer

God, grant me the serenity to accept the things I cannot change,

The courage to change the things I can,

And the wisdom to know the difference.

Living one day at a time, enjoying one moment at a time;

Accepting hardship as a pathway to peace;

Taking this world as it is, not as I would have it;

Trusting that You will make all things right if I surrender to your will;

So that I may be reasonably happy in this life and supremely happy with You forever in the next.

Amen.

Prayer of Dedication and Usefulness

God, so draw my heart to you,

So guide my mind,

So fill my imagination,

So control my will,

That I may be wholly yours, utterly dedicated unto you;

And then use me, I pray you, as you will,

And always to your glory and the welfare of your people.

Amen.

Prayer for Recovery

God, you minister to all who come to you;

Look with compassion upon all who through addiction

have lost their health and freedom.

Restore to us the assurance of your unfailing mercy;

Remove from us the fears that beset us;

Strengthen us in the work of our recovery;

And to those who care for us, give patient understanding and persevering love. Amen

Prayer for Another to Relieve Resentment

May you be at peace,

May your heart remain open,

May you awaken to the light of your own true nature,

May you be healed,

May you be a source of healing for all beings.

Bibliography

Alcoholics Anonymous World Services, Inc. *Alcoholics Anonymous.* New York: A.A. World Services, Inc., 1976.

Alcoholics Anonymous World Services, Inc. *Twelve Steps and Twelve Traditions.* New York: A.A. World Services, Inc., 1981.

Alcoholics Anonymous World Services, Inc. *The Language of the Heart.* New York: A.A. Grapevine, Inc., 1988.

Alcoholics Anonymous World Services, Inc. *The Best of Bill.* New York: A.A. Grapevine, Inc., 1990.

Barks, Coleman. *The Book of Love.* New York: HarperCollins Publishers, 2003.

Barks, Coleman. *The Essential Rumi.* New York: HarperCollins Publishers, 1995.

Foundation for Inner Peace, *A Course In Miracles.* Glen Ellen, CA: Foundation for Inner Peace, 1992.

Hanh, Thich Nhat. *The Miracle of Mindfulness.* Boston: Beacon Press, 1976.

Hooper, Walter, ed. *The Business of Heaven: Daily Readings from C.S. Lewis.* New York: Harcourt Brace Jovanovich, 1984.

James, William. *The Varieties of Religious Experience.* New York: Penguin Books, 1958.

Johnson, William, ed. *The Cloud of Unknowing.* New York: Doubleday, 1973.

Khan, Pir Vilayat Inayat. *That Which Transpires Behind That Which Appears.* New Lebanon, NY: Omega Publications, 1994.

Khan, Pir Vilayat Inayat. *Awakening: A Sufi Experience.* New York: Jeremy P. Tarcher/Putnam, 1999.

Merton, Thomas. *Thoughts in Solitude.* New York: Noonday Press, 1958.

Merton, Thomas. *New Seeds of Contemplation.* New York: New Directions, 1961.

Meyer, Marvin. *The Gospel of Thomas.* San Francisco: Harper, 1992.

Mitchell, Stephen. *The Gospel According to Jesus.* New York: HarperCollins Publishers, 1991.

Rilke, Rainer Maria. *Book of Hours,* translated by Anita Barrows and Joanna Macy. New York: The Berkley Publishing Group, 1996.

Rogers, Carl. *On Becoming A Person.* Boston: Houghton Mifflin Company, 1961.

Wilson, Colin. *Poetry & Mysticism.* San Francisco: City Lights Books, 1969.

Welwood, John. *Love and Awakening.* New York: HarperCollins Publishers, 1996.

Order Form

To order additional copies of this book, please send a check or money order made payable to

Awakened Recoveries
P. O. Box 48
Richmond, MA 01254
www.awakened-recoveries.net

Individual book copy price is $13.95. Quantity orders for five books receive a 10% discount, and orders for ten or more books receive a 20% discount off the individual copy price. Please include your mailing address and contact information with your order and add shipping and handling charges of $2.50 for single orders, and $1.25 per book for multiple copy orders. Allow two to three weeks for delivery.

Gregg D. may be reached at the above address for questions or inquiries concerning his workshops and week-end recovery retreats creating the safe space for an experiential opening to the spiritual path revealed in the Twelve Step recovery program leading to a spiritual awakening.